"Ted Siedle is a master when it comes to forensic investigations and over decades in the legal trenches, he has seen it all. In writing a best-selling book about pensions with him last year I saw not only his tenacity but his talent for cutting to the chase, for seeing the real story... for taking no prisoners. His experience, his legal expertise, his sharp analytic skills, and a hard dose of reality make *How to Steal a Lot of Money—Legally* a fascinating read and a statement on one my favorite exercises in studying life and money: Standing on the edge of the proverbial 'coin' so we can clearly see both sides... and learn from all of it."
—Robert Kiyosaki, author of the international bestseller *Rich Dad Poor Dad* and co-author of *Who Stole My Pension?* with Edward Siedle

"With the U.S. Treasury Department recommending 'mandatory' financial-literacy courses for college students, teaching how Wall Street steals is a sure way to engage readers young, as well as old. A complete education should include learning the way things really work in the real world, not just how they are supposed to work in a perfect world."
—Robin Rayfield, President, Ohio Retired Teachers Association (ORTA)

"Every government worker, every American Federation of State, County and Municipal Employees (AFSCME) member, needs to understand how Wall Street scheming undermines their retirement security. As Siedle says in the book, "Either study bad behavior and be forewarned, or risk losing everything you own."
—J. Michael Downey, President, American Federation of State, County and Municipal Employees, Council 94 Rhode Island

"Learning about investment scamming at the highest levels will help workers, including SEANC's 55,000 members, defend themselves and their families in the life and death struggle that plays out every day between investors and Wall Street. After 30 years spent investigating Wall Street looting over $1 trillion from investors, forensics expert Edward Siedle certainly is most qualified to write about the subject."
—Ardis Watkins, Executive Director, State Employees Association of North Carolina (SEANC)

How to Steal a Lot of Money —Legally

A practical guide to investment scamming
by the nation's leading financial crime investigator,
former US Securities and Exchange Commission attorney,
and record $78-million whistleblower-award winner.

Clueless crooks go to Jail
Savvy swindlers go to Vail

Edward Siedle
Based upon true events.

Foreword by Curtis Loftis
State Treasurer South Carolina

HOW TO STEAL A LOT OF MONEY—LEGALLY
Clueless Crooks Go to Jail, Savvy Swindlers Go to Vail
by Edward Siedle
1. BUS036000 2. EDU013000 3. LAW083000
ISBN: 978-1-949642-75-9
EBOOK: 978-1-949642-76-6

Cover design by LEWIS AGRELL

Printed in the United States of America

Authority Publishing
11230 Gold Express Dr. #310-413
Gold River, CA 95670
800-877-1097
www.AuthorityPublishing.com

"There is value in studying stealing. You can learn as much from studying investment scamming as you can from traditional financial literacy programs. Why? Because so much of what passes as financial advice is, in fact, a bogus money-grab."

—Edward Siedle, forbes.com

"I am the youngest CEO of an alternative asset management firm in the world. Learn about my story. If I can do it you can do it too."

—Mark Malik@wolfhedge

Moazzam "Mark" Malik, 33, stole more than $1 million from investors starting in 2011, according to a 2016 Securities and Exchange Commission final judgment. The former waiter, New York Police Department traffic agent and security guard, who claimed to be a $100 million hedge fund manager, went to great lengths to avoid giving investors their money back, including telling an investor he had died of a heart attack, authorities said.

"You are engaged in a life-and-death struggle with the financial services industry. Every dollar in fees, expenses, and spreads you pay them comes directly out of your pocket. If you act on the assumption that every broker, insurance salesman, mutual fund salesperson, and financial advisor you encounter is a hardened criminal, you will do just fine."

—William Bernstein, The Investor's Manifesto

If—

If you can devise a scheme,
Built upon foolish dreams;
That transfers wealth of others to you,
Dollar-for-dollar—patiently over time,
Without conviction of any crime;
You'll never go hungry,
Or be on the run;
Yours is the Earth and everything that's in it,
And—which is more—you'll be a con man, my son!

(Apologies to Rudyard Kipling)

TABLE OF CONTENTS

FOREWORD

When Ted Siedle called to tell me about this project, he began by saying, "Two things I know about you, Curtis. You despise corruption, and you're passionate about financial literacy. I've got just the book for you." Okay. He had my attention.

I, of course, knew that Ted had ferreted out his share of corruption. Over his 35-year, career beginning with the United States Securities and Exchange Commission, he investigated and exposed many Wall Street thieves who routinely – and often legally - pocketed investor money. His work earned both a distinguished Whistleblower Award and the respect of many people like me.

But still, financial literacy? As the elected Treasurer of South Carolina and the administrator of a program that seeks to create Master Teachers of Financial Literacy in K-12 schools, I am keenly aware of how devastating a lack of financial knowledge can be. But what had Ted learned on Wall Street that would help bolster the dearth of financial literacy in America today, and would people really want to read about it?

Once I received a copy of the book, I knew. People will not only want to read about it, they have to read about it - because Ted's book isn't simply telling people how to become financially competent. It's showing them how to become financial pros.

How to Steal a Lot of Money – Legally operates on the premise that you can't win the game if you don't know the rules, and its fascinating tales of corruption prove that the "rules" are not the rigid, set-in-stone concepts we expect them to be. Ted should know. He learned the rules from the best to ever play the game.

They were Wall Street quarterbacks who knew the "rules" so well they could bend them, twist them, stomp on them and sling them around.

The result is a master's class in financial literacy that even those of us with the smallest of investments needs to take. It helps us understand who and what we're dealing with not only to avoid being ripped off, but also to win the game.

How to Steal a Lot of Money – Legally teaches the "rules," the exceptions and all the nuances in-between that up to now, only the insiders and investment swindlers knew. It shows us how to accumulate wealth while avoiding the snares and pitfalls laid out by a host of unscrupulous scammers. The result is a lesson for the modern-day everyman that none of us can afford to ignore.

With *How to Steal a Lot of Money – Legally*, Ted Siedle has given us the cheat codes for a Wall Street win, and those of us who hate corruption and champion the little guy are cheering loudly from the cheap seats.

About the author: *Curtis Loftis was elected State Treasurer of South Carolina in 2010. As Treasurer, Loftis serves as the "state's banker," managing, investing and retaining custody of more than $60 billion in public funds. He also serves as the Chairman of the Board of Financial Institutions, the administrator of the state's Future Scholar 529 College Savings Plan, Palmetto ABLE Savings Program and the South Carolina Unclaimed Property Program.*

A national advocate for greater accountability, transparency and fiscal management, Loftis has championed a number of causes, including public pension reform, modernization of treasury, banking and investment operations, financial education in K-12 schools and most recently, Operation Check Reduction, which reduces the state's reliance on paper checks in favor of more efficient, secure and cost-effective electronic payment methods.

PREFACE

"Ask this man to dinner, you gonna have to feed him," I replied to the man on the phone with a laugh "and it's got to be Maxwell's Chophouse in Boca Raton."

Maxwell's had a terrific mahogany-paneled piano bar, soft lighting, and allowed cigar smoking. Add in an expertly crafted Manhattan cocktail on the rocks, a top-notch, thick, marbled charbroiled ribeye steak, and a band playing Sinatra live—that's about as close to heaven as you're going to find in South Florida, in my opinion.

The glow of one night at Maxwell's has never faded over the passing years. Twenty-two years ago, my foolish heart had led me to anxiously arrange with the maitre d' in advance to have a waiter deliver on a silver platter a once-in-a-lifetime offering to my dining companion. Along with the dessert I had ordered for the breathlessly charming, lovely young woman I was very much in love with, was a black velvet box concealing a diamond engagement ring.

Upon presentation of the ring, the pianist and the singer, on cue, performed the Jerome Kern and Dorothy Field lover's classic, "The Way You Look Tonight."

> Some day, when I'm awfully low
> When the world is cold
> I will feel a glow just thinking of you
> And the way you look tonight

The plans and dreams of that magical night have become reality: an artistic, lively home on the beach for a family with two children—each more brilliant than the diamonds in my wife's ring—and an aging couple still very much in love. Framed in our cabana bathroom leading to our dock is this truism:

"If you're lucky enough to live by the ocean, you're lucky enough."

While we're as stressed as any modern family and often forget to be thankful, we have, indeed, been "lucky enough."

For sure, Maxwell's Chophouse is pricey. But since my pal Duncan on the telephone had just asked me where I wanted to be taken for dinner and evidently was prepared to pick up the tab—that was his problem, not mine.

Still, I wasn't sure this kid could afford it. "Are you seriously going to fly all the way from Nebraska to South Florida, to take me to dinner? Maxwell's ain't cheap and I eat—not to mention drink—A LOT."

"Mr. Siedle," Duncan said (always profusely respectful), "if you can set aside an evening to meet with me, I'll be there—in a heartbeat. Don't worry about the cost of the dinner. Your time is more valuable than any meal. I owe you far more than you can imagine," he said.

"Plus," he teased, "I've got a surprise that's really going to blow your mind."

A surprise for me? That was refreshing, as well as intriguing. If you're going to lure me into a seemingly pointless meeting with you, by all means promise me an unexpected treat. What surprise could this young man—who I figured to be in his late twenties—have for me? Was this devout, fundamentalist Christian cornhusker giddy about having just bought his first tractor or, better still, getting married? If so, that was really, really great news he should be sharing with his family, or someone else who might give a fuck—anyone but me.

I had grown fond of Duncan over the months we'd been writing and calling one another but, in fact, I'd never met him in person.

Getting to know Duncan had started out innocently enough—he'd been an enthusiastic reader of a series of articles I was writing.

Fifteen years ago I was asked by an editor at *Forbes*, to whom I had been a source on dozens of stories related to Wall Street thievery, to become a regular contributor to its emerging online magazine, forbes.com. I've written hundreds of *Forbes* articles since then and somewhere along the way I inadvertently crossed the line, entering the confusing world of modern-day media.

I'm not a journalist who gets paid to write about matters as an observer or non-participant. I mostly write about my professional wanderings—what I uncover in my forensic investigations of investment scams. Since I'm one of the few experts who regularly undertakes these extraordinary reviews—which I refer to as "autopsies"—and the only one who writes about them, I've developed an audience of millions of readers.

In recent years, I have become well-known for my commentary on pension and other big money investment scams involving household names. I don't write, study, or care about rogue penny stockbrokers or petty hucksters. These two-bit swindlers, in the words of country singer-songwriter Dolly Parton, "ain't worth killin'."

The investment industry, as well as the limited media cheerleaders that cover it (such as CNBC) would have the public believe that most people and firms in the business of investing other people's money are honest and that scammers are the rare exception—the few bad apples.

That's simply not true.

People in any business involving handling other people's money are, first and foremost, human. If trusted with other people's money long enough, they will sooner or later succumb to the temptation to take some for themselves.

Count on it. And when they do, they often make far more money—faster—than they would by earning it honestly.

It's Human Nature to Steal

People in any business involving handling other people's money are, first and foremost, human. If trusted with other people's money long enough, they will sooner or later succumb to the temptation to take some for themselves.

Don't get me wrong. Fighting high-end financial crime can pay very well, too, and thankfully I've earned what most would consider a fabulous amount of money over the course of my career. I've been blessed many times over financially. But Wall Street criminality pays a whole, whole lot better and more fortunes have been made from scamming than from legitimate investment activity. At times it really pisses me off to see bad behavior rewarded far greater than the good.

I could easily live with the fact that doing the right thing will never pay as well as stealing. What really stings is the acrimony and thanklessness of the herculean effort required to remedy wrongdoing. It's a lot easier to lose money than it is to get even some of it back, and people rarely appreciate the messenger who tells them that the advisor they have entrusted with their savings is a cheat. Lying hucksters are generally well-liked by their clients—at least initially—or they wouldn't have been granted access to client money to later steal. Victims grimace when I ask uncomfortable questions that, if truthfully answered, will expose there is a weasel in the room.

Don't forget that the Madoffs of the world are smooth-talking, natural-born salesmen hawking feel-good pedicures and massages everybody wants. They make what I call "the happy sale." They flatter their victims and pander to their dreams. "Yes, this low-risk investment will produce enough income to easily support the retirement lifestyle you've always dreamed of. It's a rare opportunity reserved for successful, wealthy people like you who deserve the very best. Leave your money with me, go take a long cruise around the world, and call me when you get back."

I, on the other hand, often feel like a shrill voice peddling excruciatingly painful colonoscopies which no one wants. I'm offering nightmares—not dreams. I make the "*un*happy sale." I tell clients: "Not only has this so-called "low-risk" investment which seemed almost too-good-to-be-true not earned the high returns promised you, but half of your life savings are gone—either carefreely spent by you (thinking you had more money than you really did) or pilfered by your financial adviser. Now pay me if you'd like to find out exactly what happened and whether it's possible to get even some of the money back. The party's over, sober up."

So, in 2012, I had decided it was time to take a break from railing about Wall Street thievery and write a series of brutally truthful articles in *Forbes* celebrating—as opposed to bemoaning—the inescapable conclusion that intelligent financial criminals often do very well indeed. It was time to openly embrace shining reality, as opposed to continue cursing the darkness, I reckoned. In March of that year, I wrote the first in a series of articles for *Forbes* entitled, How to Steal a Lot of Money. I wasn't sure how popular the series would be or how long it would run but I figured I'd write about the subject in installments whenever time permitted.

One of the weird things about my forensic work is that there can be long periods of downtime, when seemingly not a single client in the whole wide world wants me to investigate their particular millions or billions or even trillions of dollars in jeopardy. One month I can be on a roll—a minor celebrity appearing at press conferences, on talk radio, and television; the next I'm feeling like an under-employed nobody.

The brilliant fictional detective Sherlock Holmes, who was not a regular drug addict, resorted to cocaine and morphine during periods when he was idle—having no case at hand—in protest against mental stagnation.

I'm no drug-crazed Sherlock. I've learned that in order to be an effective investigator, I have to control both my enthusiasm—(i.e., question my strongest instincts or hunches until all the facts come in), as well my discouragement—(i.e., be mindful that positive outcomes I have not envisioned may emerge from the wreckage). Dramatic mood swings need to be held in check to survive the rollercoaster ride of forensic investigations.

Downtime can be maddening for the over-active mind and is precisely when one is most likely to do something stupid out of desperation. Writing the "How to Steal" series would, I figured, keep me out of harm's way—at least free from self-inflicted harm.

The first article began with the following provocative statements:

"It's been said that crime does not pay and that cheaters never prosper. Neither of these statements is true and you should not be dissuaded from a life of theft by such homilies. History is replete with examples of people who have done very well for themselves by stealing from others. Vast personal fortunes have been amassed using illegal, ahem, business practices. Call them "robber barons" or aggressive capitalists, many were criminals. Furthermore, since financial crimes involving the greatest sums of money are rarely reported (for reasons we'll get to later), crime pays far better than historical accounts would suggest."

With those words, I began to teach *legal* thievery.

After reading the first article of the series in *Forbes*, Duncan had contacted me with some questions.

To be brutally honest, Duncan was the only reader to comment on the first article. Reader response to my highly unusual column was hardly overwhelming. Hundreds—not the thousands, or tens of thousands of readers I had expected—viewed it.

His first short message to me came in an email a month after publication.

"Mr. Siedle, your How to Steal a Lot of Money article was fascinating, not to mention very entertaining. Is another article in the series coming out soon? If not, why not? Learning about how Wall Street wheels, deals, and steals is very interesting to me. The public deserves to learn about the industry practices that undermine their financial security and, as far as I can tell, you're the only one writing about scamming at the highest levels."

I try to respond to all the rational reader comments I receive (ignoring the crazies), and like any performer, I was more than willing to speak to the only member of the audience I knew to be applauding.

I replied to Duncan thanking him for his comment and assured him I was busily working on the next article in the series.

I lied.

In fact, I was so disappointed in the reader response to the first article that I was considering dropping the idea of a series. Screw it—it was a waste of time, I figured.

But Duncan wanted to learn more from this frustrated Master of Thievery and lost little time firing more questions at me. A few days later I heard from him again.

"Thanks for the quick response. Glad to hear you'll be coming out with a new article soon. I have a few questions if you do not mind. I have read your article dozens of times. I was particularly intrigued by your statement that "If you can come up with a far-fetched idea that transfers the investor's wealth to you dollar-for-dollar, legally, you'll never go hungry." Purely for entertainment purposes, could you give me a detailed example of how such a scheme would operate? I am not in the investment business, I have no connections to the industry, but I love the thought that an Average Joe, like me, can emulate the Wall Street pigs.... Thanks for the "Entertainment."

Clearly, Duncan, like most of America, needed no convincing that Wall Street was both greed-driven and no friend to investors. While there was a time (pre-1980s) when most Americans didn't have investment accounts or buy stocks and bonds, today, Duncan knew, everyone is forced into the market. What else are you going to do—put your savings in a bank Certificate of Deposit earning 1-2 percent? Investors have no choice but to invest or gamble in stocks. But after the dot com bust and housing bubble burst, and

Wall Street and COVID-19 bailouts, everyone knows the market is rigged. Not just a little rigged—totally corrupt.

Duncan was not a believer in conspiracies generally but the evidence of systematic fraud spanning across the financial markets was and is indisputable. Connect the dots—the myriad scandals—and it's irrefutable that widespread manipulation by insiders is possible and is happening.

Perhaps the single most disturbing feature of Wall Street is the fact that when dealing with the major investment houses, all but the dumbest of investors know full well that they are going to be taken advantage of, yet feel helpless to do anything about it. Unlike bovines in a cattle car on the way to the slaughterhouse, most humans strolling down Wall Street sense danger. There's a feeling of impending doom like when dealing with a smarmy car salesman.

An institutional client of Goldman, Sachs once confided to me, "I know Goldman's going to fuck me, I just want them to tell me when and how much it's going to cost me." With billions at his fingertips, even this professional money manager felt powerless to stop the abuse.

Duncan grasped an important lesson from my first class at the online University of Stealing—a lesson I had only begun to learn myself: The story of how Wall Streeters successfully steal from investors is obviously depressing. Lives are ruined. It's a gut-wrenchingly painful human tragedy. Yet these twisted tales involving greed, scams of seemingly infinite variety, and all-too-predictable outcomes, are also entertaining.

While truth is often stranger than fiction, investment fictions are the strangest of all truths.

Investment tall-tales are often larger than life itself.

Who would believe one of the nation's largest state investment funds would be so spectacularly stupid as to invest $50 million of workers' disability money in a scam involving collectible toys stuffed with plastic pellets called Beanie Babies?

Sound far-fetched? It happened at the multi-billion-dollar Ohio Bureau of Workers Compensation a few years ago, despite my stern warnings to the state officials running the fund.

"The state of Ohio had a mess on its hands when the world came tumbling down on Tom Noe, the disgraced GOP fundraiser and rare coin dealer who was convicted of twenty-nine felony counts including racketeering, theft, and forgery in the Coingate scandal.

The state sought how best to squeeze as much as possible out of the coins, sports trading cards, historical documents, and, yes, Beanie Babies that Noe had invested $50 million of the state's Bureau of Workers' Compensation money."[1]

In the end, only one of the bumbling state fund managers got jail time for the "Coingate" (aka Beanie Baby) debacle.

Better still, I had begun to realize that the more I appreciated the entertainment value of the nonsensical, bizarre behavior I encountered in my daily work, the less enraged I felt. If you can't control the roller coaster, just sit back and enjoy the ride.

Duncan "got" that investment follies offered a rich vein of entertainment gold to be mined. When Duncan confided that he loved the idea of being able to copy "Wall Street pigs," I knew exactly what he meant.

The world often appears to be divisible into two camps. On one side are the honest, law-abiding innocents with whatever savings they've scraped together through hard work, or luck. On the other are the powerful, often corporate, savvy insiders laser-focused upon separating workers from the fruits of their labor. Understanding the tricks rich and powerful investment insiders use to sucker others is quite an accomplishment. Better still, if you can actually replicate the ruses on your own, you join the lofty ranks of the financial wizards, i.e., the puppet masters who pull invisible strings that ensnare others below. Your mastery

---

[1]   https://www.cleveland.com/metro/2012/03/the_beanie_babies_
and_other_co.html

of the art of thievery permits you to saddle, harness, mount, and ride the wealth-devouring savage stallion into the sunset.

Duncan wanted a sneak peek at Wall Street's secret play-book—to have a fair chance to make money like the vampires at the largest investment powerhouses.

That's why he contacted me.

He knew I'd been on Wall Street, that I was well-versed in the rules of the game and had even helped write the playbook. Half the battle, Duncan rightly figured, is finding someone with the knowledge you seek. Harder still is getting the individual with the requisite expertise to share what he knows with would-be victims, as opposed to using insider tricks to his own financial advantage.

Understanding the tricks rich and powerful investment insiders use to sucker others is quite an accomplishment. Better still, if you can actually replicate the ruses on your own, you join the lofty ranks of the financial wizards, i.e., the puppet masters who pull invisible strings that ensnare others below.

Your mastery of the art of thievery permits you to saddle, harness, mount, and ride the wealth-devouring savage stallion into the sunset.

Duncan and I kept communicating generally by email and occasionally by phone. He pressed me for another installment in the series.

I had always figured the How to Steal series might develop a cult-like following, given its perverse nature. After all, teaching people how to be bad, or how bad people succeed in garnering riches, was just twisted enough to appeal to an underground crowd. Interest was clearly building in the series but slower than I had anticipated.

By May, about two months after the original How to Steal article in *Forbes*, I noticed that the number of readers had sky-rocketed to more than 100,000. My articles don't usually do that—they're either a hit early-on or not at all. This was the first time I'd seen an article grow in popularity slowly over time to eventually become one of my most widely read. The time was ripe to write the second part in the series, I figured.

My second article advanced the hypothesis that there was a perfect victim for every crime and offered suggestions as to how to find the ideal victims. I wrote, "Identifying victims who will never report the crimes, or come after you for their money requires a bit of twisted logic. Do such suckers really exist? You bet they do, and once you apply common sense to defining the perfect victim, you'll soon be coming up with more potential pigeons that I ever imagined."

By late 2012, opportunities related to investment forensics—the field of study I had painstakingly pioneered for decades—suddenly exploded thanks to two newly-enacted federal so-called "whistleblower" programs.

Following the 2008 financial meltdown and the Madoff Ponzi scheme scandal, in July 2010, the Dodd-Frank Wall Street Reform and Consumer Protection Act was signed into law. Under the new law, the US Securities and Exchange Commission and the Commodity Futures Trading Commission created programs which provided for substantial monetary awards—up to 30% of any monetary sanctions collected—for whistleblowers who submitted tips to the agencies related to violations of the federal securities and commodities laws. While I had been informally providing information to federal regulators for over two decades about hundreds of cases involving wrongdoing I had uncovered in my investigative work, now these agencies theoretically could—for the first time—pay me handsomely for my insights.

Given that SEC and CFTC investigations can take two to four years to complete, there were no awards made in these programs' first years of operation. Not surprising, the whistleblower programs attracted little attention early on. The first

SEC whistleblower award was made on August 21, 2012, to a whistleblower that provided documents and information relating to an ongoing multimillion-dollar fraud. The whistleblower received $50,000, which represented thirty percent of the amount the SEC had collected at the end of the fiscal year. That was not a particularly sizable award but in 2012 it brought to my attention the two federal programs that would eventually pay me—three years later—a record-breaking award of $78 million.

Since I was busy filing my first whistleblower case, a full year passed before I published my third article in the How to Steal series in mid-2013. This final article introduced the concept of "bleeding," which involves skimming, or taking all or most of the return earned from other people's money slowly over time. Bleeding, when coupled with the "power of compounding," I explained, could result in a complete transfer of wealth from victim to huckster. Best of all, the scam I detailed in the article was and is perfectly legal. Indeed, such scams are increasingly commonplace as Wall Street has migrated from traditional investments (like mutual funds) to the costliest, highest risk, most-secretive investments ever devised—such as hedge funds and private equity funds.

As I wrote and published the above two follow-up articles in the series over the course of eighteen months, Duncan and I continued to develop a long-distance relationship of sorts. Still, we lived thousands of miles and worlds apart.

I live life in the fast lane—Boca Raton, a tropical paradise that is so notoriously appealing to unsavory stockbrokers that state securities investigators nationally dubbed the area "the Maggot Mile" in the early 1990s. In 2014, the *Wall Street Journal* reported that the neighboring town of Delray Beach had one of the highest clusters of stockbrokers with regulatory red flags—(bad disciplinary records)—in the country.

Hustling has long been a problem in Florida, gradually evolving from land-boom swindles in the 1920s to drug-dealing coupled with money-laundering in the 1980s to bogus penny stock scams in the 1990s, to Ponzi schemes, hedge fund scams, mortgage and health care fraud, and online gambling through today. Like slime mold growing on the glass of a tropical fish aquarium, the fungus crept up the coast from Miami to Fort Lauderdale and then to Boca—where it took hold and has thrived for more than two decades.

Boca is a beautiful seaside community consisting of twenty-seven square miles of beach, fairways, and Bermuda grass, planned during the 1920s by California-born architect—Addison Mizner—as a major resort destination. The pink Mizner designed Mediterranean Boca Raton Resort which opened in 1926, still defines Boca architecture and luxury style.

Not only is Boca the home of many dubious companies and habitual swindlers, further straining the community's social fabric is the profound lack of large corporate employers. There are very few legitimate jobs to be had in this tropical oasis where seemingly everyone, whether they can afford it or not, wants to lounge.

You might say that Duncan hailed from a town that is the opposite of all things Boca.

I gathered from his open, folksy manner that Duncan lived in a quintessential small town in Nebraska where folks knew, and neighbors watched out for, one another. Don't get me wrong—even remote parts of America are not immune from Wall Street or home-grown investment scams. For example, around the time the Madoff scam was exposed, about 200 Nebraskans lost more than $100 million in the largest Ponzi scheme in state history to a firm based in his hometown that specialized in selling insurance to Native Americans but also sold other investments.[2] Tailor-made affinity fraud.

Duncan told me he was very much involved in his community and especially his church. He was clearly driven to get ahead and had a keen interest in investing. But from what I could gather through our limited conversations he was not remotely

---

2   https://journalstar.com/business/g-i-insurance-agency-lo
st-millions-in-investments/article_2477be1a-5c29-5a21-aca7-
3f760746d702.html

dissatisfied with his life in a small town and did not yearn for the bright lights of the big city. He was comfortable with the environment he was born into where folks thought kindly of him and had always treated him well. I'd say he seemed to want to do something special or remarkable—but in his own backyard. Unlike most of us restless Americans, he knew where he belonged.

I knew where Duncan came from; less clear to me was where he was aiming to go or how I figured into his plans.

Duncan was an over-eager learner who peppered me with questions for as long as he could keep me on the phone or computer. If I ever were to be a teacher, I'd want to have a roomful of students just like him—wildly motivated, hanging on my every word—disciples who were absolutely certain that I and I alone possessed the wisdom they sought. If only the rest of the world genuflected to me as Duncan did.

I was more than curious to meet Duncan that balmy South Florida night in September 2013 for the dinner at Maxwell's he had invited me to. I was looking forward to it.

I arrived at the steakhouse forty-five minutes early for one reason. If I'm going to smoke a cigar, which I don't often do, I want to have the time—as much as an hour—to enjoy it. I don't want to be rushed into ordering appetizers or a meal.

Besides, Duncan was no client of mine and as far as I knew we had no real business to discuss. I was doing him a favor. This was more of a social call—a rare night out without my wife and kids—a chance to shoot the breeze with an admiring fan.

I was seated at a corner table with my back to the wall so I could watch the crowd, when Duncan hurried in. A tall, thin, physically fit, clean-cut young man wearing an olive-green suit and carrying a garment bag—it had to be him. He recognized me immediately from my picture in *Forbes*.

"Sorry I'm a little late," he said as he reached over to shake my hand. "I had trouble finding a taxi at the Fort Lauderdale airport."

"Dude, you did *not* have to wear a suit for me," I joked. "And what's that thing hanging around your neck like a noose?"

For the occasion, I had showered, shaved, and put on a starched shirt, and slacks—none of which is routine for me these days. I usually just roll out of bed and go to the office in sneakers, khaki shorts, a T-shirt, and baseball cap.

Duncan was visibly excited and upbeat. When the waiter asked whether he'd like to order a drink, I wasn't surprised to hear him order fruit juice and to learn he didn't drink alcohol. This guy was way too focused and lacking in frustration to resort to drinking. Still, I appreciated that he made a point of encouraging me to enjoy my drink. He wasn't going to ruin the night by preaching to me.

"Please, enjoy yourself, Mr. Siedle. After all, we're celebrating."

"Call me Ted, please," I said, "even if I am old enough to be your father. Now, what is it we're celebrating? What's this mysterious surprise you have for me?"

"Well, let me start by giving you this gift—a token of my appreciation for all you've done for me," he said. He handed me a crisp, thin white envelope.

"Thanks," I said nonchalantly as I sipped my Manhattan on the rocks and drew on the cigar. *Probably a card with a gift certificate tucked inside,* I thought. I laid the envelope on the starched white tablecloth, figuring I'd open it later.

"No—open it now," he said in nervous anticipation.

As I opened the envelope, I could see there was no stock Hallmark card there, just a folded piece of plain white stationery paper on which was handwritten in blue ink, "For the Grandmaster Shyster, from a grateful student."

Wrapped in the paper was a cashier's check made out in my name for $100,000.

"So, what's this?" I said, going along with the joke.

"It's a check for $100,000 ... and it's real," said Duncan.

"Believe it or not, I did it," he proudly stated.

"You did what?"

"I put together an investment fund and raised a total of $10 million through my church and community," he said. "Once I persuaded the church to invest the initial $100,000 and allow me to mention its participation in selling the fund to others, everyone else in the community jumped in.

It's an investment scheme—just like ones created by big Wall Street firms that you described in your articles. The way I structured it, it will pay me 7% a year, come rain or shine—a wealth transfer—like you advised. Since I'll be making more than $700,000 per year for the next decade, I decided to give a portion of my earliest earnings to you by way of thanks. You've certainly earned it."

At this point a number of different thoughts and emotions were stirring within me.

Is he serious?

Is he nuts?

What am I doing hanging out with this idiot?

On the other hand, if this is for real, that's pretty cool.

Did we actually do this? Pull it off?

Why am I saying "we?" I had nothing to do with this scam.

Or did I?

Of course, I did. This hick didn't have a clue about investment scamming before he met me.

"Mr. Siedle, assuming I followed the model you provided correctly and according to your projections, I should be able to pocket an amount equal to my clients' total investment capital within eight years, right?"

Son of a bitch.

Duncan had it done it right. The fees I had built into the model, invested and compounding over an eight-year period would net him a cool $10 million. He was on his way to vast riches. And since he had carefully followed my instructions— never once breaking the law—he was going to be free to enjoy his newly-created wealth.

He was going to Vail—not jail.

What he didn't know yet—because I hadn't told him—was that if he followed my instructions faithfully, I projected that within twenty years he'd be worth an astonishing $50 million.

"I could never have done this without you," he said excitedly.

"Well—why the hell *did* you do it?" I asked with a stammer.

Duncan explained that he wanted to show that anyone can do what Wall Street does and in so doing, expose the hypocrisy.

Wall Street wants the world to believe that only a handful of highly-accomplished Ivy League graduates at the biggest, most powerful firms are capable of constructing sophisticated financial schemes—schemes that even investors whose money is at risk will never understand. Wall Streeters also believe that since they're uniquely skilled, they're entitled to steal from others.

Most of us are reluctant—either out of shame or embarrassment—to take the last cookie from a party platter in a crowded room. We were taught by our elders—at home, in church, and in schools—to be considerate, compassionate, and to think of others. In a room full of polite folk, the last cookie rarely gets eaten until the party's almost over. Wall Street goons, on the other hand, will grab and gobble the last cookie, then move on in search of more goodies—snickering at the dullards who were "too slow" to seize the obvious opportunity.

Members of the "greed breed" believe (perhaps because they have been taught as much at elite schools or by their employers) that they are *uniquely entitled* to the best life has to offer—the moment they see it—without hesitation. Even without having to "earn it." Laser-focused, selfish, and unencumbered by pangs of conscience, Wall Street's greed breed has a distinct advantage in the race to riches.

Duncan believed if he could show that anyone—even a hick from Nebraska—could replicate the chicanery, then the whole argument that Wall Streeters are especially entitled to the riches falls apart. He wanted to cut to the chase and learn to steal like Wall Street without growing up privileged, attending an Ivy League college, and then working at a major financial institution for warm-up. "Just teach me what I need to know to unseat the ruling class," was all he asked.

Change the world by mirroring it? Sounds like something a Zen master would say. Who knows—it might just work, I thought, staring at the fresh, wholesome face in front of me.

Remarkably, this young man, both by meticulously following my instructions and his own bold, reckless action, had proven my mastery of thievery. In a perverse sort of way, he'd validated my life's work. Maybe my peers had failed to appreciate the value of my forensic work over the decades, but his generation "got it"—and ran with it.

Who would have ever imagined that I, the unwitting teacher, would be thankful a "student" had gone rogue and used my knowledge to produce real results in the real world? Then again, isn't that what teaching is all about?

Duncan was the first successful graduate from my online University of Scamming.

But instead of my handing him an embossed diploma of uncertain value after years of hefty tuition payments, upon graduation he handed me a fat check—my cut of the ill-gotten gains related to his scam.

An education the student pays for, if and only if he succeeds—what's wrong with that?

Parable of the Last Cookie

Most of us are reluctant—either out of shame or embarrassment—to take the last cookie from a party platter in a crowded room. We were taught by our elders—at home, in church, and in schools—to be considerate, compassionate, and to think of others. In a room full of polite folk, the last cookie rarely gets eaten until the party's almost over. Wall Street goons, on the other hand, will grab and gobble the last cookie, then move on in search of more goodies—snickering at the dullards who were "too slow" to seize the obvious opportunity.

Members of the "greed breed" believe (perhaps because they have been taught as much at elite schools or by their employers) that they are *uniquely entitled* to the best life has to offer—the moment they see it—without hesitation. Even without having to "earn it." Laser-focused, selfish, and unencumbered by pangs of conscience, Wall Street's greed breed has a distinct advantage in the race to riches.

1

I CAN TEACH YOU TO LIE, CHEAT, AND STEAL A LOT OF MONEY—LEGALLY

I can teach you to lie, cheat, and steal *a lot* of money—billions—legally.

I've done it before and I can do it again. I am confident that with my help, you *can* do this.

Over the course of my thirty-five-year career I have pioneered the field of forensic investigations of the business of managing money. I've spent a lifetime studying the greatest swindlers—many of whom no one has ever heard of because they never got caught. On the other hand, some of the most dangerous actors are well-known, highly respected, global financial institutions whose thievery has never been fully exposed.

These days when I'm asked to explain what I do for a living in terms anyone can understand, I say: "It's like the television show *CSI: Miami*. Each episode typically opens with the discovery of a dead body and the job of the forensic investigators is to figure out whether the death was due to natural causes or foul-play. In my work, the 'death' I'm investigating is a dead, or seriously sick, investment. Someone has lost money—lots of it or I wouldn't have been called in. The immediate question is, did the investment fail—was the money lost—due to natural causes (such as an unforeseen decline in the stock market), or was there foul-play?"

More often than the general public or even victims ever imagine, the damage is caused by wrongdoing—unethical, self-dealing financial advisers who drain client accounts for their own benefit. I regularly uncover massive scams and widespread business practices that are harmful to investors, not adequately disclosed and, at best, poorly understood by victims. Undisclosed conflicts of interest; hidden, excessive and illegal fees; and other violations of law—crimes rarely exposed or prosecuted—are all forms of thievery we'll be talking about in this book.

It's a wealth transfer game these investment con men and women play: Your wealth gets transferred to them.

To date, I've investigated over $1 trillion in investment schemes and uncovered hundreds of billions successfully stolen without a gun or whimper from the victims.

For my efforts, in 2018, I secured the largest whistleblower award in history from the Commodity Futures Trading Commission—$30 million and in 2017, the largest award from the US Securities and Exchange Commission—$48 million— both related to a $367 million JP Morgan Chase settlement that charged the bank with failing to disclose certain conflicts of interest to some of its wealth management clients. In 2016, I obtained the first whistleblower award in history from the State of Indiana. But these were not my first whistleblower experiences by a long shot.

Early in my career, in 1988, I uncovered longstanding illegal trading activity at my Wall Street employer which I fully investigated and confidentially reported to the FBI and SEC. These reported illegalities remained secret for the next fifteen years until I was subpoenaed by then-New York Attorney General Eliot Spitzer. When the wrongdoing by senior management was finally made public in 2003, there was a run on the bank. My former firm's assets under management plummeted from $400 billion to $192 billion and the firm was fined $150 million—the largest fine in the history of the asset management industry at that time. The firm has never recovered its once stellar reputation.

There are a million ways to make a million but few as remarkable (and unlikely) as getting paid by law enforcement or regulators for protecting investors from Wall Street greed.

Theft of the magnitude I'm talking about may be hard for you to believe. The scamming is happening all around you—you just aren't aware of it because you don't know what to look for and because it's actively concealed by the perpetrators.

It's probably not surprising to hear small investors often lose their meager savings to fraudsters. But, as you will learn, some of the supposedly most "sophisticated" investors in the world—massive multi-billion-dollar pensions set aside for state and local government workers, corporate pensions sponsored by Fortune 500 employers, and investment funds established to manage the wealth of sovereign governments—lose the most (in dollar terms) to scams. Wealthy and sophisticated investors are not immune to the onslaughts of thievery.

In this book, we'll begin by discussing some of the fundamentals of fraud, such as the optimal times and places for scamming, as well as mundane skills would-be investment scammers may need to master. These include how to create a compelling fake resume; how to look rich—when you're not; how to pick the perfect victims; how to get victims to willingly hand over their money without the use of force; how to manipulate and misrepresent—inflate—investment performance results; and how to cryptically disclose to investors your worst deeds so you don't wind up in jail.

We will analyze some of the largest, most complex, and least understood financial scams ever created—exotic investment schemes, like hedge and private equity funds, as well as fund of funds and fund of funds of funds, which are far removed from most people's financial lives.

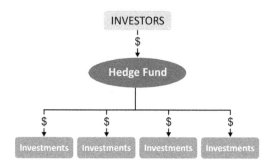

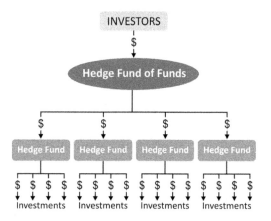

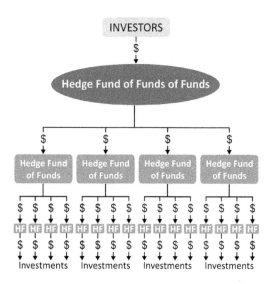

However, we'll also look at seemingly noncontroversial commonplace investments, such as mutual funds and 401ks, which have a reputation for being safe and well regulated. We'll see how billions are systematically stolen out of these investments as well.

Whether it's hundreds of thousands and millions pilfered on Main Street or tens of billions on Wall Street, the premise of this book is simple:

There is value in studying stealing.

You can learn as much from studying investment scamming as you can from traditional financial literacy programs. Why? Because so much of what passes as financial advice we'll see is, in fact, a bogus money-grab.

> There is value in studying stealing.
>
> You can learn as much from studying investment scamming as you can from traditional financial literacy programs. Why? Because so much of what passes as financial advice is, in fact, a bogus money-grab.

Wall Street thievery, you will learn, touches almost everyone and the financial impact is staggering.

401K SCAMMING

For example, since the 1980s, corporations have been eliminating pension plans established to provide retirement security for their employees and pushing employees into 401ks. Today, most American workers invest in the stock market through mutual funds offered in 401k savings plans. 401ks are a popular employee benefit because employees can use the plans to put pre-tax compensation towards their retirement, maximizing their contributions. Employers may also match the funds employees contribute, further enhancing the tax advantages of a 401k.

All that sounds good, so where's the "dark side" or scam?

For openers, 401k savings plans have, for decades, been misleadingly sold to workers by employers and Wall Street as "retirement" plans which provide retirement security comparable to pensions. That's bullshit.

401ks were never designed to replace pensions and the forecasts backers of these plans have used to sell the plans to employees have long been outrageously deceptive.

In April 2011, I stood with over 200 City of Atlanta police officers jammed into a crowded committee room at city hall for a workshop held by the finance committee of the city council. By the end of the tense four-and-a-half-hour marathon session, hundreds of other city employees had lined the corridors watching the closed-circuit broadcast on television monitors throughout the building.

The workshop was an opportunity for the police to present their response to a proposal by the mayor to "freeze" their pension benefits and force city workers in a 401k-type plan. In other words, city officials had come up with a scheme to reduce the pension benefits promised to employees in response to looming budget deficits. All that remained was for the city to convince workers the proposed 401k-type plan—which would save the city hundreds of millions—was every bit as good as the old pension.

It wasn't...and the cops knew it.

The police had passed around a hat and collected cash donations amounting to a few thousand dollars to pay for me to fly to Atlanta and speak on their behalf at the committee meeting—as their expert, disputing the recommendations of Wall Street experts hired by the city.

I explained to the city council that America was facing a retirement crisis. Corporations closing their mismanaged pensions and forcing their workers into deeply flawed 401k plans to save corporate dollars was largely to blame.

With median 401k balances for sixty-five-year-olds at around $70,000 nationally, it's no secret that the great 401k experiment of the past fifty years has robbed tens of millions of workers. Who can live on the returns $70,000 in savings will produce—say $300 a month? How many people do you know that are confident their 401k will adequately provide for their retirement needs?

The 401k wreckage we are witnessing today was avoidable had our elected representatives and regulators protected investors from financial services industry greed.

Instead, corporations saved a ton and Wall Street made boatloads of money from shifting workers' savings from pensions to 401ks. Corporations cut their pension liabilities and Wall Street got to charge workers exponentially greater fees for managing retirement assets in 401ks. They won.

Workers were thrown to the wolves, forced out of pensions which paid fees of less than half a percent into the poor performing retail mutual funds offered in their 401ks that charged fees four-times greater, say two percent. They lost. Workers paid far more to Wall Street each year and were left with a whole lot less savings for their retirement.

401k plans now hold more than $9 trillion in assets. And pensions are nearly extinct in the private sector.

Even the former head of the American Society of Pension Actuaries, Gerald Facciani has stated, "The great lie is that the 401(k) was capable of replacing the old system of pensions... It was oversold."[3]

WEALTH OF HARD-WORKING TRANSFERRED TO WEALTHY, HARDLY-WORKING

Beginning in 2006, I was involved, as a lawyer and consulting expert, in the initial wave of class action lawsuits alleging excessive fees and mismanagement at many of America's largest 401k plans, including Walmart, Boeing, Northrop Grumman, Kraft, Edison, Caterpillar, Deere, United Technologies, General Dynamics, ABB, and International Paper. As I dove deeply into the structure of these mega-401ks and examined prevailing industry practices, I

---

[3] https://www.cnbc.com/2017/01/04/a-brief-history-of-the-401 k-which-changed-how-americans-retire.html

was shocked to discover that the financial institutions entrusted with workers' savings had entered into agreements amongst themselves to share money skimmed from workers' accounts—without telling workers. The Fortune 100 corporate sponsors of these 401ks and, in a few rare cases, the investment firms picking workers' pockets, paid dearly to settle the class action lawsuits brought on behalf of plan participants. Sadly, these cases were brought too late for at least two generations of workers who began investing in 401ks in the 1980s.

While workers were shocked to learn that the largest, supposedly most sophisticated corporations in America had looked the other way while Wall Street ripped-off their 401ks for nearly three decades, revelations that smaller corporate plans fared far worse were less surprising.

Most— ninety-five percent—of the nation's 401k plans are puny. These plans have less than $5 million in assets. Typically, the employers who sponsor teeny plans get sold the worst deals offered by Wall Street bottom feeders. These 401ks offer uncompetitive investment options that gouge workers with fees as high as three percent annually. Corporations that offer high-cost, poor performing crappy saving programs are doing their employees no favors. With stocks expected to return only six percent annually over the next two decades, Wall Street is pocketing fully half the gains workers can expect on their savings. That means workers end up with half the retirement savings they would have accumulated by retirement in a well-designed plan.

The wealth of the hard-working gets transferred to the wealthy, hardly-working.

As a result of widespread litigation over the past fifteen years challenging the abuses and growing awareness, 401k looting had been waning. Workers had been getting a better deal. The fees paid to Wall Street had been coming down. Not anymore. Now fees are poised to skyrocket.

Wall Street's solution to failing 401ks—and every investor problem—is always the same: Pay us more in fees.

In 2020, Trump's US Department of Labor granted permission, for the first time, for Wall Street wolves to sell the highest cost, highest risk, most secretive investments ever devised by Wall Street to 401ks. 401k investors will be devoured like lambs to the slaughter. Bad enough that DOL—the federal agency which is supposed to protect corporate retirement plans—welcomed the wolves of Wall Street to feast on workers' hard-earned savings, but the explanation the agency provided for its reckless action was perverse.

> Wall Street's solution to the failure of 401ks—and every investor problem—is always: **Pay us more.**

Ramping up the fees and risks to 401k savers will "overcome the effects the coronavirus has had on our economy" and "level the playing field for ordinary investors," said Trump's DOL. The chairman of Trump's SEC agreed that allowing workers to gamble their limited retirement savings like millionaires who can afford to lose lots amounted to "COVID relief."

Trust me—gambling is no way for anyone to improve his or her retirement security.

PENSION LOOTING

The damage caused by Wall Street looting corporate pensions, as opposed to 401ks, is far more obvious. Wall Street merely bleeds workers' 401ks by skimming a few percent a year. 401ks injured by the skimming limp along, never performing to their full potential.

Pensions, on the other hand, get brutally murdered by Wall Street. They die. Over the years I've learned a lot about Wall Street devious practices which cause pension "deaths" from my forensic investigations. I firmly believe every dead pension deserves an autopsy.

Approximately 5,000 corporate pensions which had promised retirement security for millions of private sector workers have been killed in recent decades. The carcasses of these pensions have been dumped at the doorstep of an agency of the federal government, the Pension Benefit Guaranty Corporation. Despite repeated cries from workers and retirees who have seen their retirement benefits slashed by fifty percent or more, no one has *ever* fully investigated who or what caused these thousands of unanticipated deaths.

Were pensions looted and, if so, by what means, who profited and by how much? We know who lost—workers and retirees. Who won?

Neither the private corporations which sponsored the pensions, nor the PBGC—which ensures the retirement security of more than 35 million men and women participating in pensions—want workers to learn what caused their pensions to die. That's more than a little difficult to understand given the fact that PBGC has accumulated an overall deficit of $50 billion+ from helping private corporations walk away from pension corpses.

Wall Street merely **bleeds** workers' 401ks by skimming a few percent a year. Pensions, on the other hand, get **brutally murdered** by Wall Street. They die.

I met with PBGC officials on multiple occasions beginning in 2005 (accompanied by a platoon of union and Congressional staff members) when United Airlines' four pensions—which were then underfunded by more than $10 billion—were permitted to be terminated in bankruptcy and dumped onto the agency. (The United pension terminations remain to this day the largest liabilities that PBGC has taken on under the federal pension insurance program.) When I explained the agency could recover billions by holding the looters responsible, the bureaucrats balked. Nobody wanted to go after the looters.

Unlike PBGC, participants in failed pensions—workers and retirees who have seen their retirement dreams turn into nightmares—want answers. However, they have neither the money nor access to documents necessary to launch their own investigations of the looting and file lawsuits to recover funds.

Six years after the United debacle, in 2011, 5,200 members of the US Airline Pilots Association hired me to conduct the only forensic investigation ever undertaken of a failed pension trusteed by PBGC—the US Airways Pilots pension. PBGC had refused the union's repeated demands for an investigation. The multi-billion-dollar Pilots' pension, I discovered to my amazement, had never been audited. While I was not permitted access to the overwhelming majority of the pension's documents, I was able to unearth longstanding Wall Street looting of the pension—looting which had escalated as it careened into bankruptcy.

Again, Wall Street's solution to the dying US Airline Pilot's pension had been: pay us more fees for riskier investments. Throwing lots of costly Hail Marys, as recommended by Wall Street neither improved performance nor saved the pension—only Wall Street's bottom line benefitted. Worse still, I discovered that consistent with PBGC practice, records related to the looting had been "buried" along with the pension when it died. The federal agency cannot investigate Wall Street pension thievery even if it wants to—PBGC does not maintain custody of potentially incriminating records once a pension folds. So, the lesson here is if you're going to steal from a corporate pension, best to kill it so that no one can ever piece together the evidence and come after you.

You'd think that those responsible for destroying the retirement security of millions of private sector workers would be held accountable. Looters almost never are. So, scammers should have no fear.

As we'll see, trillions in state and local government workers' pension plans are even more susceptible to looting as a result of lack of effective state regulation, politicization of investment decisions, and corruption. Kindergarten teachers, sanitation workers, firefighters, and cops lacking any training in financial matters, sit on the boards of these pensions that Wall Street targets for it sketchiest, priciest deals. Even when they are well-intentioned (and they often aren't), these boards are easy prey for hucksters. My estimate is that over $1 trillion has been skimmed by Wall Street from public pensions.

Learning how the Ivy Leaguers legally loot government workers' pensions can mean future riches for you—if you choose the scamming life.

REGULATORY CAPTURE

Better still than the news that a savvy investment swindler can make a fortune is the fact that if you steal smartly—legally—you'll never go to jail.

We'll discuss why you need not fear federal and state regulators or law enforcement.

Banking, securities, and investment advisory regulators have all been "captured" by the financial services industry. These regulators smugly do exactly as little as they're supposed to—just enough to keep the suckers at the poker table, i.e., "maintain investor confidence," but never call out the cheaters and seriously jeopardize Wall Street profiteering.

Most of the information financial firms are required by law to maintain for regulators to inspect on a regular basis, as well as records noting legal deficiencies uncovered by regulators—all of which are required to be kept for the "protection of investors"—shall never made available to the public, regulators and the regulated agree. Why should information, gathered in the name of "investor protection" be kept from investors? Makes no sense.

The political pressures brought to bear upon the SEC are widely known but rarely is the extent to which these political factors undermine the overall effectiveness of the Commission openly discussed. It is accepted practice that political leanings play a formidable role in the selection of SEC Commissioners. For example, it is unheard of for an individual, Republican or

Democrat, with a record for fighting on behalf of investors and opposing the financial services industry to be selected as a Commissioner. Don't expect to see Ralph Nader appointed as an SEC Commissioner in your lifetime. Persons whose careers have involved representing financial services firms or employment with such firms are the usual suspects. Below the Commissioner level, the selection of Division Directors within the agency is also influenced by candidates' acceptance with the regulated. In summary, selection of senior management at the SEC is not determined by merit using investor protection accomplishments as the yardstick; rather, a favorable reputation with the regulated is of greater significance. The speed with which these government managers find comfortable quarters within the industry after their period of "government service" is powerful evidence of how seldom they seriously oppose the regulated. Public confidence in regulators, which reached an all-time low with revelations regarding Madoff's $65 billion Ponzi scheme during the depths of the 2008 market meltdown and Wall Street bailout, has yet to recover. Indeed, the Trump administration was intent upon undermining government oversight and confidence in regulators once-and-for-all.

Law enforcement, we'll see, is so clueless when it comes to investment wrongdoing that cops themselves often fall victim to investment scams.

SECRECY SCHEMES AND SKIMMING DEVICES

Scamming at the highest levels involves bizarre business practices, understood by few which are deliberately shrouded in secrecy by the perpetrators—practices which are, frankly, so seemingly nonsensical that they may be hard to believe.

I'll explain how, over the past decade, Wall Street has been successfully sweeping hundreds of billions of US investor assets into secret offshore accounts, not only to avoid paying taxes, but also to conceal all sorts of questionable dealings, including outright theft. It's all been accomplished perfectly legally—with the consent of the investor-victims. Every scammer needs to understand the benefits of operating in secrecy, as well as how to persuade investors to consent to a lack of transparency regarding their investments.

I'll also show you how Wall Streeters have structured investment scams around the country—in Kentucky, North Carolina, and Rhode Island—so that they get paid tens of millions annually **for doing nothing.** Does getting paid $14 million, $30 million, or a mere $4.5 million a year for doing nothing appeal to you? While getting paid millions for not doing a damn thing may sound like the very definition of fraud, I'll explain how it's done legally.

The 401k, corporate, and government pension scams introduced above are broad examples of what I call perfect crimes: big money heists never prosecuted. These are widespread thefts, involving hundreds of billions, even trillions of dollars and tens of millions of investors. The stealing is known and periodically spotlighted in the media—for sure, in my *Forbes* columns—yet nothing is done to stop it. Rarely are any of the culprits prosecuted or fined and even when they are, no one ever admits guilt or goes to jail.

Yet investment wrongdoing does far more financial harm than all other criminality combined, globally. That's why it's so critical you understand the various forms of scamming and how it's done. Whether you're looking to join in the thievery or guard against it, you need to know about it.

While you will find a heavy dose of sarcasm and humor in these pages, this book is no joke. The information provided on the art of investment scamming is accurate and the forensic insights are well-founded, based upon decades of professional experience.

Better still, in the Supplementary Reading Materials section I have included Forbes.com articles I have written which further discuss the issues raised in the chapters, as well as an actual expert forensics report from a public investigation I undertook involving over $8 billion.

So, take the book seriously.

Do I really want you to go out and ruin people's lives by lying, cheating, and stealing their hard-earned lifesavings? Of course not.

When men, women, and families are victimized by financial criminals, it's devastating. People lose their sense of safety, control, self-worth, and even purpose. It happens far, far more often than you might believe.

While forensic and fraud accounting experts estimate that the cost of fraud globally amounts to trillions annually, the true figure is exponentially greater. The overwhelming majority of investment scamming is not included in global estimates because fraud experts with accounting backgrounds are not trained to identify the myriad forms of scamming and aren't looking for it.

For example, the forms of harm to investors I focus upon are not generally factored in the overall damage calculations by accountants focused upon numbers alone.

My estimate—based upon decades of experience—is that well over *half of all investing* involves scamming of one sort or another.

I hope that through learning the art of investment scamming at the highest levels—implicating many of the world's most respected and trusted (and therefore most dangerous) financial institutions—you'll be better equipped to defend yourself and your family in the life and death struggle that plays out every day between investors and Wall Street.

Stopping fraud globally is an impossible task. On the other hand, defining and exposing scams that pose the most serious risk to your overall wealth-health is doable, and in this book we'll do just that. Let's call this a "gonzo course in financial literacy" or "financial literacy on steroids."

A complete education should include learning the bad and the ugly—not merely the glorious and meritorious. The student should be taught what is, not merely what should be—the way things really work in the real world, not how they are supposed to work in a perfect world.

Lying, cheating, and stealing are so commonplace in life generally, and in the world of investing especially, that they are **not** the exceptions. Scamming mercilessly overwhelms any so-called rules and devours those who play by them. So, learning "rules" without learning the even greater larcenous "exceptions" makes no sense—it's reckless. Schools and professors who teach the "rules" alone are negligent, in my opinion and put students, at a minimum, at a competitive disadvantage, or, worse still, in harm's way.

An education which ignores, or excludes, the study of pervasive repugnancies only ensures certain unscrupulous insiders will continue to be able to blithely manipulate and mislead the clueless masses, depriving investors of their hard-earned savings and undermining confidence.

For the student of investing, the choice is simple—either study bad behavior and be forewarned, or risk losing everything you own.

Lying, cheating, and stealing are so commonplace in life generally, and in the world of investing especially, that they are **not** the exceptions.

Scamming mercilessly overwhelms any so-called rules and devours those who play by them. So, learning "rules" without learning the even greater larcenous "exceptions" makes no sense—it's reckless.

Over *half of all investing* involves scamming of one sort or another.

And, now for the mandatory disclaimer in bold print:

This book has been written for general informational purposes only, and is not intended to provide, and should not be relied on for tax, legal, investment, or accounting advice. You should consult your own tax, legal, financial, and accounting advisors before engaging in any transaction. The author assumes no responsibility or liability for any error or omissions

in the content of this book. The information contained herein is provided on an "as is" basis with no guarantees of completeness, accuracy, usefulness, or timeliness. In no event will the author be liable to you or anyone else for any decision made or action taken in reliance upon the information in this book or for any consequential, special, or similar damages, even if advised of the possibility of such damages.

2

MY FIRST ENCOUNTER WITH A VELVET-THROATED INVESTMENT HUCKSTER

According to the Consumer Financial Protection Bureau, financial services companies collectively spend about $17 billion each year on marketing, which amounts to about $54 a person per year. **That figure does not include marketing of retirement products, college loans, and investment products, which involve exponentially greater sums.** With over $26 trillion in mutual funds which charge an average of one percent in sales commissions alone, hundreds of billions of dollars are spent by Wall Street selling investment products to unsuspecting Americans. Legions of well-groomed marketers and silver-tongued salesman are employed in nationwide schemes to persuade investors to hand over their hard-earned savings.

The CFPB also looked at how much is spent on financial education in America. Not surprising—it's a whole lot less than the amount spent on marketing. America spends only about $670 million on financial education, or about $2 a person per year.

Lastly, virtually nothing—perhaps only a few million dollars annually—is spent on in-depth investigations into why investment products promoted by Wall Street all-too-often fail to deliver the promised results.

What I call "autopsies" of dead or dying investments almost never happen. Rather, there is broad acceptance that investing often results in losses for which no one is to blame.

Advertising or selling investments is intended to entice you to buy the product. Forensic investigations of investments focus upon the structure of the product, the integrity of ongoing management, and the performance results. Often, with so-called "toxic" investments, we determine that the management and structure is so seriously flawed that the investment is virtually guaranteed to fail.

For example, there are certain investments which charge fees so high that it is impossible the investor will ever end up with more than a minimal return on his money. The investment scammer has designed the product to enrich himself no matter what; the investor will be lucky to get his principal back over time. Other products incorporate corrupt business practices that ensure the investor will be disadvantaged.

Standard industry practices, established by industry, are intended to benefit…the industry.

In summary, vastly more money is spent and vastly more money can be made from selling dubious financial products than can be made from investigating and addressing the harm these products cause. Further, absent forensic investigations that ferret out wrongdoing, financial education efforts will always be incomplete and fail. You cannot teach investors to avoid doomed investments if you don't fully understand the mechanics of the scam and can explain it to potential victims.

So, how did I come to specialize in forensic investigations of the most massive investment frauds—pioneering a field of study that barely exists, offering a service that people rarely want?

> **Vastly** more money is spent and vastly more money can be made from selling dubious financial products than can be made from investigating and addressing the harm these products cause.

My initial face-to-face with a polished investment swindler was a year before I graduated from law school and began work at the US Securities and Exchange as a newbie regulator. It was my first week as a summer intern in the SEC's dreary government-grade cement grey offices not-so-scenically situated on Causeway Street, in the shadows of the elevated Interstate 93 Expressway and commuter rail line in downtown Boston.

I sat squeezed between two grown-ups (Commission lawyers) in a cramped windowless interior conference room for a deposition of Robert Defeo, an investment adviser who had gambled and lost a chunk of the endowment of a local Catholic college he had been hired to oversee.

His roll-of-the-dice bet on a wildcatting Australian oil and gas limited partnership had ended with only one pip on each die—snake eyes. Defeo was accompanied by two pricey Ivy League lawyers from one of Boston's most venerable law firms he had retained to defend him.

Unlike common thieves, when crooked investment scammers get caught, they often have plenty of pluckings from their client pigeons stashed to fund their defense. Let that be a lesson to all would-be fraudsters: set aside a portion of your ill-gotten gains for a dedicated defense fund. A tough defense will keep most victims, regulators, and law enforcement at bay. It's simply a cost of doing business.

Defeo was in his fifties, distinguished, gray-haired, wearing tortoise shell horn-rimmed glasses and a heavy brown tweed suit in summer. He was no typical New England Brahmin—more likely, he charmed the school administrators claiming to be a devout Italian Catholic.

Defeo was the very picture of a trustworthy financial adviser. As a fifty-something year old mentor of mine gleefully commented when I was just starting out, "In this business, the more gray hair you have, the more clients trust you. That's one more reason to love the business of managing money—no mandatory retirement age."

Defeo was impressively educated, holding two PhDs from a prestigious Canadian university—one in philosophy and the other in medieval studies.

At the time, I thought it was remarkable that anyone held an advanced degree in a field as obscure as medieval studies. In the decades since, I've never met anyone else boasting such a credential.

> Successful scammers set aside a portion of their ill-gotten gains for a dedicated legal defense fund. A tough defense will keep most victims, regulators, and law enforcement at bay. It's simply a cost of doing business.

Given his love of storytelling, perhaps spending six years studying the crusades, castles, knights, and princesses made perfect sense. Then again, maybe claiming to hold a doctorate degree in a very off-the-radar field of study was a tall tale calculated to mildly impress clients but not so grand as to arouse suspicions. Brilliant. I wondered: Did anyone ever ask the subject of his dissertation?

The fact that professionals in the investment advisory industry had such broad intellectual curiosities was encouraging to this stifled law student. Unlike the oppressively narrow constraints of law (aka "legal reasoning"), the investment world seemed full of opportunity for free-range, imaginative thinkers.

Defeo was neither nervous nor remorseful under questioning. There was no sweat on his brow as he patiently explained to us hayseeds in the room why gambling the conservative college endowment in a highly speculative oil and gas limited partnership was, in fact, the epitome of prudence. He was confident he could, like a master alchemist, turn lead into gold bewitching the government lawyers in the audience. They had never witnessed powers such as his, he knew.

Defeo's contorted reasoning went something like this:

In the late 1970s, inflation was one of the most significant problems facing the Carter administration, peaking at 13%. Runaway inflation meant that the real value of investments was eroding at a comparable rate. In order to merely preserve the value of the endowment, said Defeo, it was necessary to invest in assets which had an expected rate of return in excess of 13%. The wild-ass Australian oil and gas deal offered the possibility of such a double-digit return.

In an era of outrageous inflation, investments which seem to be highly speculative are, in fact, conservative, claimed Defeo. Black is, in fact, white, my friends.

The SEC lawyers in the dark cave-like room neither applauded nor snickered at Defeo's grand finale—they just looked tired as they silently, dutifully scribbled notes on their yellow legal pads. It was just another day—another emotionless drill. There were no distraught victims with tears streaming down their anguished faces pounding the table screaming for justice. No perpetrator repenting his sins or pleas for mercy from the gallows.

No gallows.

The law review articles assigned as reading that summer introduced me to the notion that this different class of criminal—investment scammer—deserved to be treated specially.

Jail time for common crimes any moron can commit makes perfect sense and should be mandatory. Society exacting revenge by kicking the crap out of such lowlifes serves as an effective deterrent.

Wall Street financial terrorists deserve to be punished more thoughtfully, I learned.

The readings reinforced my suspicions that harsh criminal penalties rarely make sense (even though part of me wanted to see investment weasels go to jail like everyone else). Most serious violent crimes are committed in the heat of the moment by impassioned perpetrators who aren't remotely thinking through the consequences of their actions or even necessarily intending the specific harm they cause. Death penalty for murderers is hardly a deterrent. Most non-violent crimes, such as petty thefts, involve substance abusers or impulsive youth—neither of which respond well to harshness.

Maybe common criminals deserved the same well-reasoned review of their transgressions—a punishment crafted in logic, a prosecution void of evocative images of the pain and suffering they'd caused. Heady notions of justice should not be reserved for only the most sophisticated crooks that often do far greater damage.

Should the penalty for stealing a lifetime of hard-earned savings, ruining lives, destroying generations of wealth be more or less severe than shoplifting from Walmart?

My first sniff of the pure-oxygen air of the money management industry left me almost dizzy. This was a brave new world of ideas. Here fantastic theories were spun of fine gold thread into intricate webs capturing a constellation of sparkling diamond stars.

A plausible argument could be made that gambling money donated by loyal alumni to preserve the college they once had attended and loved was righteous. And Defeo, with his persuasive skills intensely focused, was making it.

This modern-day knight looked and sounded impressive dressed in tweed armor charging at a gallop with lance at full tilt astride two white-shoe legal stallions.

I was unprepared for the nuances of this mental battle. I was a mere investment neophyte who barely knew the difference between a stock and a bond.

Mesmerized as I was by his attack, the strong stench of wretched bullshit burned my flared nostrils.

It was like watching a magic show, secretly wanting to believe but knowing it's a stinkin' illusion.

I had the same feeling decades later testifying as an expert in the Madoff case. The make-believe world Madoff had created and sustained for decades was so convincing that I had to periodically shake the pixie dust out of my hair as I reviewed thousands of pages of documents and remind myself that everything—every trade confirmation, account statement, and performance report produced over the decades—was part of an elaborate lie.

The truth is that a case can be made for any absurd investment scheme by the right velvet-throated huckster. For example, if widget investments have performed horribly since the dawn of man, then this is the perfect time to invest—at the bottom of the widget market. Buy low. Widgets prices have nowhere to go but up, the scammer promises.

For many investors, the allure of spectacular investment returns is impossible to resist—regardless of whether the stated "strategy" is ludicrous. That's why Ponzi schemes which promise returns of twenty percent or more (and generally collapse quickly) are so appealing to some. On the other hand, there are investors who will be suspicious of outlandish promised results but can be lured into your scam for far less—if you've got a good "story." Madoff investors were satisfied with promises of consistent returns around ten percent annually—returns which were low enough (for certain periods even below the actual return of the S&P 500) to allow the Ponzi scheme to go undetected for decades.

But Ponzi schemers eventually go to jail and you don't want that. If you take the time to craft a clever investment tall tale and faithfully execute it, i.e., actually invest some of the money, you can lawfully deprive your investors of enough money to fly (by private plane) to Vail—regardless of the outcome. Jail or Vail, you choose.

So, watch, listen to—study—seasoned investment hustlers and learn from them. You'll find them everywhere these days on the internet, CNBC, Bloomberg News, and especially talk radio. Your goal, as a scammer, is to craft an investment sales pitch that will persuade investors to give you their money, i.e., excite their imaginations and appeal to their greed. Don't worry about whether the strategy will work or not—just whether it will sell. Once you have their money—if you structure your investment properly—you don't even have to invest it in the manner you described to would-be investors.

As Warren Buffet, arguably the world's most successful investor once said, "If there's a sucker at the poker table and you don't know who it is, it's probably you." Everyday legions of suckers flock to the stock market poised to gamble away their life savings. Scammers—make those suckers your benefactors.

Just as a plausible argument can be made for any far-fetched investment, there is a counter-argument for every proposal. The best defense against investment fraud is to construct the counter-argument as you listen to the pitch. It's easy to be a naysayer when you don't want to believe but that's not good enough. Instead, investors need to learn to turn every idea on its head and articulate the contrary thesis—regardless of how appealing the scheme may be.

Why might today be the best and the worst time of times to invest in, say, gold? Be convincing. Make the sale either way. Trust me, it can be done.

3

WHY SCAMMERS LOVE FLORIDA, COUNTRY CLUBS, CHARITIES AND CHURCHES

It is common knowledge that certain geographic *locations* are scamming hotbeds. Due to factors such as geographic beauty; concentration of wealth; elderly, retired population; lack of legitimate employment opportunity; enhanced asset protection; and lack of effective policing, fraud flourishes in some areas. For example, picturesque coastal and waterfront environments attract affluent year-round residents and care-free vacationers, as well as investment fraudsters chasing the good life and easy money.

Think *Miami Vice* and *Hawaii Five-0*.

Likewise, certain *venues* such as churches, charities, and private country clubs—located anywhere in the world—are also swindler havens. Shared religious and social values make it easy for the fraudster to spread the word about his scheme by pretending to be a member of the group.

Let's start with geographic locations ripe for scamming.

I often tell people the five Bs brought me to South Florida: blue skies, beaches, boats, beautiful women, and barbeques. Given a choice between a bonfire on the beach or Pavarotti in the Park, you'll find my toes in the sand.

The temperature and geographic beauty were paramount in my decision to move to South Florida from Manhattan in 1995. As the owner of a business with a diverse national clientele, it was of no concern to me that I had no existing or prospective clients in the state and that there were virtually no corporate employment opportunities in Florida. I moved here because I could afford to live, as well as conduct my business from wherever I wanted—not because I intended to pitch my services to members of the affluent crowd who had made their money elsewhere and brought it down south with them. Likewise, I was not drawn to the Sunshine State in hopes of pilfering the retirement nest eggs of the massive elderly population.

When I first settled here, I was surprised to meet commodities, securities, and investment advisory professionals who had relocated after being barred by regulators from these industries for their misdeeds up north in financial centers such as Boston, New York, or Chicago. These, let's call them "snow-vultures" versus "snowbirds" openly discussed without shame or remorse past exploits that landed them in hot water with regulators and law enforcement—which they commonly referred to as "misunderstandings." Most of the bar crowd singles I encountered were low-brow hustlers formerly employed by notorious retail bucket-shops I'd heard of but never done business with in my institutional investing career.

Before moving to South Florida, I had never met anyone barred from the securities industry, yet in the Sunshine State barred scammers were everywhere. Apparently as soon as these lowlifes were fired by their Wall Street employers, they'd high-tail it out of town recognizing their careers were over—at least for the immediate future. After a few years—a "time out" in South Florida—if they'd stolen so little that it hardly mattered or so much that they commanded the respect of their peers on Wall Street, they might get back in the game.

Worse case—if their securities, commodities industry, or investment advisory disciplinary histories were insurmountable—they'd set up a totally different type of scamming operation locally like selling unwanted and unneeded diabetic supplies and medical devices to Medicare patients, including the dead. Medical fraud, it seems, is as popular locally as investment fraud due to the substantial elderly population.

For example, according to the Office of Inspector General, US Department of Health and Human Services, since 2012, the government has opened 102 cases involving durable medical equipment (DME) fraud in Florida, out of a total of 822 nationally; 63 DME fraud cases have resulted in criminal actions in Florida, out of a total of 361 across the country; and the US government has recovered more than $58 million dollars from DME cases in Florida out of more than $611 million nationwide.[4]

Perhaps we're not unique (given the global decline in ethics), but in South Florida society today, most assuredly, there is no shame related to wealth accumulated through questionable or illegitimate means. As long as you've profited handsomely from your thievery, you'll be greeted with open arms, bear-hugged, and kissed wetly on both cheeks.

Investment schemers, disbarred lawyers, and medical doctors with suspended licenses and even felony convictions are all—like moths to a flame—attracted to South Florida. What's not to love—year-round sun and one of the most protective homestead provisions in a state constitution, protecting homes of unlimited value from creditors—including those purchased with criminal proceeds. Ever wonder why people like Dennis Kozlowski (Tyco), Scott Sullivan (WorldCom), and O.J. Simpson moved to Florida and bought multi-million-dollar homes? Answer: Protection of their assets.

As unwholesome and dangerous as the South Florida social milieu is today, it's only going to get worse.

A few years ago, Florida's then-Governor Rick Scott (whose role in the largest Medicare rip-off in history did not deter voters from electing and re-electing him as governor and now senator), broadly invited the newest breed of Wall Street gangster—hedge fund managers, including the good, the bad, and the ugly—to move to the state.

---

[4]   https://www.abcactionnews.com/news/local-news/i-team-investigates/insiders-reveal-secrets-of-medical-device-scam-targeting-thousands-of-floridians

I'm not so sure why our former governor, now state senator, reasoned inviting investment gunslingers would be good for the Sunshine State. It's not like these guys build businesses that hire lots of employees locally or pay taxes.

Nevertheless, according to the Business Development Board of Palm Beach County, lots of calls came in from New York hedge fund owners tired of high taxes and cold weather looking for a change. When the ethically-challenged chief executive of a state calls for fellow rodents to join him at a beach party, not surprisingly, they come scurrying.

Then-Governor Scott also very publicly invited Yale University to cast aside three centuries of tradition in New Haven, Connecticut, and relocate to Florida to avoid paying taxes—once again demonstrating his cluelessness.

In conclusion, when it comes to investment fraud remember the realtor's mantra: location, location, location. What factors may suggest that a given locale is ideal for scamming?

However, the fastest growing form of scamming—internet facilitated crimes—is perpetrated by fraudsters living far from their victims. There are certain locations like Thailand and other parts of Southeast Asia that spawn criminality because of their remoteness—lack of effective policing or regulatory oversight. From these locations, expatriate investment fraudsters can operate boiler rooms swindling foreigners living in the world's major countries without fear of prosecution.

DIFFERENT SCAMS DESIGNED FOR DIFFERENT LOCATIONS

Not only do certain areas attract scammers, frauds are often shaped by, or tailored to, the locations or communities, e.g., ethnic or retirement, where they are foisted. That is, certain scams are designed to appeal to certain people in certain places.

For example, scams targeting the wealthy often feature "exclusivity" in the sales pitch.

So, whether you're trying to reduce the risk of getting ripped off or planning the perfect scam, bear in mind that location matters. Some locations seemingly invite scammers and different scams prosper in different locations by design.

> Some locations seemingly invite scammers and different scams prosper in different locations by design.

CHOICE SCAMMING VENUES

Now let's talk about choice venues.

A favorite venue for marketing dubious investment schemes has long been exclusive private clubs. If you want to rip off the wealthy, you've got to go where they congregate and pitch them when they have their guard down—in a relaxed social environment.

Most of these clubs have rules which supposedly prohibit use of their facilities for conducting business, as well as deducting dues as business expenses. Yet Wall Street money managers and other swindlers who live in Connecticut and New York and own no homes in South Florida have confided to me that they join one or more clubs down here—1,300 miles away—strictly for marketing purposes. You'd think it would be pretty obvious to these clubs that financial hustlers who have no local residences are joining purely to prey upon their wealthy members. They ought to know better.

After all, the Palm Beach Country Club was the hardest hit of all clubs nationally by the Madoff Ponzi scheme not that long ago (2009).

For whatever reasons, enforcement of no-business policies rarely happens at private clubs. "Wealth managers" which industry insiders sarcastically call "wealth manglers" need not fear being snubbed by our local clubs.

More Wall Street hedge fund and other fraudsters moving into the state of Florida (by invitation of the governor, as mentioned above) means there will be more hustling at private clubs and, inevitably more scamming and big losers (given the lack of regulation of these highest-cost, riskiest funds). For those who might spoil the party at the country club—the scammers' marketing frenzy—it may get harder than ever to be invited, I wrote in *Forbes* a few years ago.

Little did I suspect when I wrote the article that my family would soon be spurned by a private beach club near my home.

Over the years I'd grown used to my neighbors who were members of the club joking that if I ever did apply for membership, I'd never be admitted because I'd successfully investigated some of its more prominent members. Members had been publicly disgraced, fired from their jobs, and sued for fraud because of me. Granted, that might make for a few awkward moments poolside sipping cocktails, but I assumed my margarita-soused neighbors were kidding during these conversations—after all, they were laughing.

Turns out, the mother-chucklers were deadly serious.

After ten years of living on the beach, when I finally did apply to the private club (with the requisite number of member sponsors, having met all stated membership criteria, and after a personal interview), I was apparently rejected for that very reason I was told by a friendly board member. (I say "apparently" because the club, it seems, doesn't tell applicants why they've been rejected or, in my case, even that I had been rejected.)

Hunt for ducks in their natural habitat.
The wealthy can be sitting ducks in their natural habitats, i.e. private country and beach clubs.

Don't be shy, be discrete.
Private clubs are regularly used for marketing (aka "networking") by doctors (especially plastic surgeons), lawyers, and financial advisers. You'll never be the only pool-side hustler.

Join multiple clubs to maximize your marketing reach. While the membership dues may be steep, access to a well-healed crowd lounging with its guard down is worth the price of one or more private club admissions.

Churches, charities, and other non-profits are also choice venues for scamming because when fraudsters pretend to share the understandings, interests, or beliefs of the group, members trust them.

Investment scammers often make large well-publicized donations to charitable organizations upon joining in hopes of being entrusted with organizational funds or member assets. For example, a money manager might graciously donate $1 million to a non-profit center for the arts, in hopes of being hired to manage $75 million of the center's endowment. In addition to the endowment, the strategic donation introduces the scammer to other wealthy donors who can be solicited to manage their personal assets.

For example, in 2006, the Madoff Family Foundation, which listed $20 million in assets, reportedly gave away $1.2 million. Ironically, giving away *stolen money* was the price Madoff willingly paid to *continue stealing*.

Financial advisers hovering around non-profits and making donations as a precursor to fleecing is so obvious that it's hard to believe this scam still works. It does. Charities jump at sizable donations and brush aside any lingering concerns about donor motives.

Then there are affinity fraudsters that prey upon members of identifiable groups, such as religious or ethnic communities, the elderly, or professional groups. The fraudsters who promote affinity scams frequently are—or pretend to be—members of the group. They may enlist respected leaders from within the group to spread the word about the scheme by convincing them that a fraudulent investment is legitimate and worthwhile. Many times, those leaders become unwitting victims of the fraudster.

Because of the tight-knit structure of many groups, the SEC admits it can be difficult for regulators or law enforcement officials to detect an affinity scam. Victims often fail to notify authorities or pursue their legal remedies and instead try to work things out within the group. Where the fraudsters have used respected community or religious leaders to convince others to join the investment, victims are inclined to accept reassurances from those leaders. The Nebraskan Native American home-grown insurance Ponzi scheme referred to earlier was specifically designed for that particular community, as was the Ponzi scheme below targeting the Haitian community in New York busted by the SEC.

SEC Charges Adviser for Running Ponzi Scheme Targeting Haitian Community

Washington DC, Nov. 6, 2019

The Securities and Exchange Commission today filed charges against a New York investment adviser for operating a multimillion-dollar investment club that was actually a fraudulent Ponzi scheme targeting members of the local Haitian community as well as his family and friends.

The SEC's complaint alleges that Ruless Pierre ran an investment club called the Amongst Friends Investment Group that operated as a fraudulent Ponzi scheme. From at least March 2017, Pierre allegedly raised over $2 million from at least 100 investors, predominately Haitian New Yorkers, who purchased high-yield promissory notes through Amongst Friends. As alleged, Pierre induced investors by promising unrealistically high rates of return of at least twenty percent every sixty days. In reality, the complaint alleges that Pierre incurred heavy losses trading securities and concealed them by using new investor funds to pay older investors and issuing false account statements showing investment gains. Pierre allegedly further financed the fraud by using money that he embezzled from a former employer to make interest payments to investors.

The SEC's complaint also alleges that Pierre fraudulently raised at least $375,000 from more than fifteen investors related to a scheme involving the sale of partnership interests in a fast food chain. In or about November 2018, Pierre began to sell partnership interests in a fast food franchise, with agreements that falsely guaranteed monthly returns of ten percent (sixty percent per year) plus quarterly profit sharing. As alleged, at the time he sold these interests, Pierre knew that the franchise could not provide sufficient profits to pay investors the promised returns.

As an example of fraud within a religious community:

"William Neil 'Doc' Gallagher, who once wrote a book called *Jesus Christ, Money Master: Four Eternal Truths for Personal Power and Profit*, hosted retirement planning programs on local radio in the Dallas area. He said he had a 'mission' to be 'a vehicle of God's peace and comfort to as many people as possible, helping first with their financial peace of mind, then also with their spiritual, emotional, and family well-being.' He sold 'guaranteed income' products to people in their sixties and older, says the SEC.

"From 2014 until earlier this year he raised somewhere between $19 million and $29 million, the SEC says. Today: There's just $821,951 left.

"Gallagher could not immediately be reached for comment."[5]

In closing, if you're looking to reduce your risk of getting defrauded, watch for and beware of country club and charity hustlers. On the other hand, if you're a scammer, give serious consideration to private clubs, churches, charities, and other non-profits in planning your scam. The cost of joining these organizations can be steep but well worth it. And, once you've stolen millions, don't hesitate to—like Madoff—make big charitable donations if that's the price you have to pay to steal millions more.

---

[5] https://www.marketwatch.com/story/americans-have-some-disturbing-misconceptions-about-their-financial-advisers-2019-03-14

4

GETTING VICTIMS TO WILLINGLY HAND OVER THEIR MONEY

S uccessful big league investment scamming—which is our goal—has four defining characteristics.

First, a *lot* of money must be involved in the scheme and a lesser amount—but still a *lot*—stolen. Second, the victims must *willingly* hand over their money to the scammer. This is not a book about robbery or the taking of money by force, threat of force, or by putting the victim in fear. Besides, robbing people makes it more likely you'll get caught—go to jail, not Vail. Third, money preferably should be *imperceptible pilfered* which generally means stolen slowly over time. Fourth, and most important, the perpetrator must *not get caught*, or, if caught, she must not get prosecuted. These are the geniuses you rarely hear about because, unlike Madoff, they don't get exposed, prosecuted, and imprisoned.

Four defining characteristics of the perfect investment scam:

A *lot* of money must be stolen.

Victims must *willingly* hand over their money to the scammer.

Money should be *imperceptibly pilfered* slowly over time.

The scammer must *not get caught, or if caught, not prosecuted.*

Getting victims to willingly part with their money can be relatively easy. Position yourself to routinely handle other people's money and before you know it, some of their money will become yours.

Financial advisors, bankers, brokers, lawyers, accountants, realtors, and a host of other professionals are in businesses that involve people routinely handing over their hard-earned money for seemingly legitimate financial purposes, including the good, the bad, and the ugly.

Would-be scammers needn't be intimidated. Some of these professions involving high degrees of financial trust (for example, realtor, stockbroker, or investment adviser) do not require any education or degree—not even a high school diploma.

Further, in virtually every profession, there is a host of bogus certification or credentialing schemes that exist purely to enhance credibility. Pay a small fee, take an online test, and voila, you're a certified/chartered financial investment/consultant/planner/analyst/counselor/manager aka investment genius. An online search for financial certifications and licenses will reveal an alphabet soup of designations, some of which are more rigorous than others.[6]

---

[6]   https://www.investopedia.com/articles/01/101001.asp

> Some professions involving high degrees of financial trust (for example, realtor, stockbroker, or investment adviser) do not require any education or degree—not even a high school diploma.
>
> Further, in virtually every profession, there is a host of bogus certification or credentialing schemes that exist purely to enhance credibility.
>
> The goal of most certification programs is to make the candidate appear and present more credibly.

You may choose to avoid the most demanding certifications and licenses because, truth be known, consumers—even the wealthiest—generally cannot distinguish between the legitimate and utterly bogus. Your time is valuable, don't go overboard.

On the other hand, since few of these programs are expensive or particularly demanding, you may wish to accumulate a small handful of certifications. Remember that the goal of most of these certification programs is to make the candidate appear and present more credibly. If nothing else, such programs will teach you the right words to recite to wary clients and help perfect your professional sales pitch.

After all, knowledge and eventual mastery of the rules will be invaluable as you seek to successfully break them. A demonstrated knowledge of the rules—referencing them in your dealings with clients—will lead clients to trust you more.

Why do you think Madoff was active in the National Association of Securities Dealers, a self-regulatory securities-industry organization, served as chairman of its board of directors, and was a member of its board of governors?

Clothe yourself in legitimacy every chance you get.

As opposed to establishing a professional status or role that gives you an opportunity, or excuse, to handle other people's money, situations may arise when you can seek to convince others to hand over their money, regardless of your credentials or background. For example, you may get involved in an organization and then volunteer to serve as its treasurer simply based upon your popularity (and the fact that no one really wants the non-paid position).

A compelling background and resume, as well as appearing to be rich and successful, will also encourage people to believe you are trustworthy.

> Knowledge and eventual mastery of the rules will be invaluable as you seek to successfully break them. A demonstrated knowledge of the rules—referencing them in your dealings with clients—will lead clients to trust you more.

5

HOW TO CREATE A COMPELLING FAKE BACKGROUND AND RESUME

To succeed as a sophisticated investment fraudster, you will need an impressive resume and/or intriguing background to appeal to clients.

If you ain't got it, fake it.

As my dad used to say, "Twenty years after the war everybody claims to have been a colonel."

For openers, there are at least three different ways of lying about yourself that you should master:

- First, there is the old-fashion formal printed resume written in corporate-speak.
- Second, there is the rollicking brave new world of social media; and
- Third, there is the oldest form of lying—oral storytelling.

Each of these methods of communicating your expertise to potential clients requires a different level of truthiness, i.e., tolerates more, or less lying.

Lie the least on your formal resume; be more creative on social media (including having supposed "others" lie about your accomplishments—recommend your services); and, with respect to oral storytelling, feel free to make up the wildest shit you can imagine.

Ironically, the least formal lying—storytelling—may be as persuasive as the most formal, the written resume. There are three obvious reasons for this. First, if you're appropriately guarded (as a scammer should be) and diligent, hardly anyone will ever see, much less read your resume. Second, humans are hardwired to remember stories and, third, if you repeat a story enough times to enough people, it will take on a life of its own—grow in veracity.

My advice is to generally steer clear of grandiose claims, such as educational and professional credentials the suspicious can fact-check with ease. Forget about faking an advanced degree from a prestigious domestic university, or pretending to be a lawyer, or medical doctor. You don't have to aim that high or be so conventional when creating bogus achievements. Fly under the radar with creative, obscure experiences and accomplishments.

For inspiration, take a look at Operation Varsity Blues, the 2019 college admissions bribery scandal involving thirty-three parents of college applicants accused of paying more than $25 million to fraudulently inflate entrance exam test scores, fabricate sports credentials, and bribe college officials. The parents, students, and coaches falsified sailing, volleyball, rowing, water polo, tennis, and soccer achievements—all off-the-beaten-path sports with limited public scrutiny. In some cases, image editing software (e.g. Photoshop) was used to insert a photograph of a student's face onto a photograph of another person participating in the sport to document purported athletic prowess. Not surprising, none of the students claimed to be the quarterback of their high school football team—a status which could be easily verified.

Make your background interesting, believable, and full of great stories.

As much as possible, do not outright lie: s-t-r-e-t-c-h the truth. Some ideas:

- Purchase bogus or low-quality credentials, designations, or accreditations that involve no prerequisites, no curriculum, no testing, and little or no continuing education.

- Purchase or create fake diplomatic-sounding titles related to distant places. How about the title of Argentinean "Chancellor," conferred by "Commander Roberto Arias," President of the Center for Buenos Aires Cultural Integration and Business?
- Claim to be a member of the large cast of a reasonably well-known ensemble Broadway production of years gone by—but never the star.

     "Did I mention I toured as a member of the cast of Riverdance—*the theatrical show featuring traditional Irish music and dance—until I tore my meniscus? It was the greatest thrill of my life."*
- Create "minor league" sports accomplishments.
- Claim to be the founder of an impressive sounding start-up that you sold for a fortune but no longer exists.

Finally, my personal favorite: Claim to be the trustee or beneficiary of a highly secretive private trust with supposedly hundreds of millions or billions in assets. If your story is intriguing enough, you can count on others to spread it for you.

In conclusion, do not resort to fraudulently claiming you have a Harvard MBA to impress others. You don't need to—besides, you'll get caught. Instead, creatively craft an intriguing fake background which will be impossible to verify, just as impressive, and far more memorable.

Remember that nothing is as convincing in drawing investors into a scam as perceived vast wealth. And while vast riches are relatively simple to voluntarily prove—Show them the money!—it is virtually impossible to definitively disprove wealth claims without access to underlying records and statements.

Think about it: Possibly the most public person in the world—the former president of the United States—was able to convince hundreds of millions of people globally for years that he was worth billions without ever once proving it—and with legions of hostile professional investigators and journalists seeking to disprove his claims. You too can do so on a much smaller scale.

> The key to creating a killer fake resume is to claim accomplishments no one can easily dispute, or verify.

6

NOTHING SUCCEEDS LIKE BEING, OR AT LEAST LOOKING, RICH

One thing is for certain: No one wants to hire a penniless pauper to manage their wealth. Who would hire a bum to advise them on how to get rich?

People believe that financial advisers who are wealthier than they are or, better still *really rich* must be successful investors. That's how these advisers got to be rich, right?

> While vast riches are relatively simple to voluntarily prove—Show them the money!—it is virtually impossible to definitively disprove wealth claims without access to underlying records and statements.

Rich advisers will create riches for them, they believe.

While that makes a certain amount of sense, wealthy advisers generally have not made their money through astute investing. Most are simply adept at making money off their clients or transferring client wealth to themselves.

"Once in the dear dead days beyond recall, an out-of-town visitor was being shown the wonders of the New York financial district. When the party arrived at the Battery, one of his guides indicated some handsome ships riding at anchor. He said, 'Look, those are the bankers' and brokers' yachts.'

"'Where are the customers' yachts?' asked the naïve visitor."[7]

Where indeed.

As Warren Buffet said in a 2016 annual letter to shareholders, "When trillions of dollars are managed by Wall Streeters charging high fees, it will usually be the managers who reap outsized profits, not the clients."

In short, investors should never assume a wealthy financial adviser is an investment sage. The standard fee structure in the money management industry provides that managers get paid handsomely, say a 1-2% annual asset-based fee, regardless of the outcome. In addition, many managers get a staggering percentage of any gains, say 20-30%. No matter how much money they lose, they get paid. And if they gamble and win big, they get really rich—billions. It's a heads-they-win, tails-the-investor-loses scheme.

The very fact that, according to standard industry practice, financial advisers are paid lavish fees regardless of whether or not they make money for their clients reveals that marketing or raising money from investors is the key to success, not investment acumen.

Nevertheless, since investors believe that rich advisers will make them rich, to be a successful investment scammer you must *appear* to be wealthy.

The classic chick-and-egg challenge is how to get other people to willingly hand over their money to you (to supposedly invest) before you've had a chance to pilfer enough client money to make yourself rich?

I didn't say you have to actually be rich—just look it. All you have to do is convince others that you are.

---

[7] Where are the customer's yachts? Or a good hard look at Wall Street, Fred Schwed Jr., 1940.

7

HOW TO LOOK
RICH AND SUCCESSFUL—
WHEN YOU'RE NOT

Thanks to technological advances, like Photoshop and social media, it's easier than ever to look attractive, rich, successful, and highly-regarded by your colleagues and clients online, as well as socially prominent even if you're actually a penniless loser.

Perception is reality, so being able to manipulate how people see you is critical. It is well worth your time to study all the tools that are available to enhance how you are perceived by others online.

Perception is reality, so being able to manipulate how other people see you is critical. It is well worth your time to study all the tools that are available to enhance how you are perceived by others online.

It is also beyond the scope of this book to do much more than draw your attention to the fact that investment scammers are already and likely will continue to be at the forefront of online reputation manipulation. Most of us are selective in our Facebook and other social media postings to convince others that our lives are possibly far more attractive and eventful than in reality. Fraudsters, on the other hand, use every technological advance to further their business purposes: ripping people off.

My favorite low-tech, on-a-shoestring "wealth-enhancers" include:

- Go to the nearest Ferrari, Bentley, or Lamborghini dealer and take a selfie sitting in a flashy car. Put the picture of you posing in "your" car on Facebook for prospective clients to see.

- Go to an executive airport and pose as close as possible to the most impressive, yet nondescript personal jet you can find. Put the picture on Facebook or, better still, your "company" website.

While I won't name the scammers, trust me the Ferrari and private jet ruses are examples from real cases I've investigated.

- Up-tech with image editing software and you can, as they advertise, "reimagine reality." A picture of you standing next to your good friends, Donald Trump or Bill Clinton may enhance your credibility and no one's ever going to ask them if they remember having met you.

- For $185.00, buy yourself a counterfeit Rolex Blue Dial Submariner that looks exactly like the real thing costing $15,000.00 and probably tells better time.

- Fake pearls and fake diamonds are difficult to identify—even for experts.

Search online and you'll find tons of articles about how to look, dress, and act like a millionaire. For example, begin by learning about expensive designer brands, cars, restaurants, foods, drinks, artists and travel destinations so you can converse easily about them and share your opinions. Armed with designer clothing knowledge, you'll be prepared to prudently invest in your future buying a few quality pieces to complete your wardrobe of affordable items. Make sure your clothing investments are well-tailored and classic so that they won't go out of style. Since shoes make the outfit, you'll need at least one pair of conservative, expensive shoes. Wear a small amount of sophisticated scents and stay away from heavy florals. Reading periodicals of the wealthy like Forbes, Barron's, and Wall Street Journal will keep you informed as to matters important to the rich.

Remember, craft your identity to appeal to the victims you have targeted. To appeal to less sophisticated victims, flashy indicia of wealth—"bling"—may be all you need. On the other hand, if you're trying to cozy-up to established wealthy folks (i.e., "old money"), you may have to be more discrete or refined in your approach. Too much bling suggests you're a poseur.

If you want to impress men or women for romantic purposes, that's a different exercise than luring in unsuspecting investors—although there definitely are some commonalities.

Setting the Stage

In the 1990s, I owned a trading firm on Wall Street and lived in Manhattan. Like every savvy New York businessman with a demanding entertainment schedule, I staked out one restaurant I would frequent with my clients. My repeat business earned me the right to personal treatment in an otherwise impersonal metropolis. The chef, bartenders, and waiters all knew me and talked me up to my prospective clients.

Whenever and wherever you pitch clients, make yourself seem more important and successful than you really are by carefully "setting the stage." Always take the pigeons to a place where you'll be greeted by name and treated like royalty. Based upon that single experience in your presence, many clients will assume that you are treated like a celebrity wherever you go.

8

FIND THE PERFECT VICTIMS FOR YOUR PERFECT CRIMES

A key component to planning the perfect crime is to coolly identify the perfect victim for that specific crime. (We'll talk about crafting the perfect crime later.)

Theoretically, there is a perfect victim for every type of crime. I don't know this for certain but intuitively I think it's true.

However, *I do know* for a fact that there is a perfect victim for major league investment fraud or theft. Fleecing grieving widows or the elderly may net you a few million and maybe, if you're lucky, they'll be too frail or scared to come after you. But if you're looking for really big money, set your sights on investors and organizations that, for any number of reasons, are not eager to go public with their accusations—such as charities; state and local government workers' pensions; and tax cheats that have a lot to lose by crying foul.

In other words, if you steal money from a charity that is concerned its donors will stop giving if the loss is made public, the likelihood the charity will publicly prosecute you, is reduced.

Then there's the "cheat the cheaters" strategy.

While testifying as an expert witness on behalf of the City of Fairfield, Connecticut, Police and Firefighters Pension fund in a 2012 case involving the Madoff scheme, I learned that some of the victims who had lost big had not filed claims with the bankruptcy trustee. Billions unclaimed? Why? These victims were foreigners who had not paid taxes in their home countries on the amounts they invested with Bernie and, therefore, could not come forward to assert a claim without risking prosecution.

If you steal money from someone who's never declared it to the taxing authorities, the chances the tax cheat will come after you are further reduced. Use the tax laws and other laws to your advantage: the more your clients have to worry about possible tax penalties or criminal fraud prosecution themselves, the less likely they'll come after you for stealing their money.

My investigations of private banks operating in the US that cater to wealthy foreigners, particularly so-called "Edge banks," led me to conclude that these banks have been able to offer phenomenally uncompetitive investment products and services to clients—to pick money out of their clients' pockets—because the clients are primarily concerned with laundering their tens of millions in gains from sales of drugs, or evading taxes. The rate of return on the assets invested is only a secondary concern to these customers. Even when they discover they've been cheated, they won't sue the bank. Clients don't sue and regulators and law enforcement in the US look the other way when these foreigners get hosed. A comparison of the minor fines banks pay, versus the massive profits they earn from laundering money should convince you that this time-tested swindle is working well for them.

I've spent most of my professional career focusing on state and local pensions—investment victims which handily win the award for least likely to report mega-thievery. These pensions are overseen by trustees that lack any investment experience and decisions about who to hire to manage pension assets are often made based upon contributions to local politicians. As a result, they are perfect prey for the wolves of Wall Street who will happily pay bribes for a license to steal. When they lose billions, public pensions are more concerned about exposing their ignorance and cultures of corruption than recouping stolen money.

Recall that, according to the SEC, in the case of affinity frauds victims often fail to report wrongdoing where the fraudsters have used respected community or religious leaders to convince others to join in the investment. Think about how you can enlist others who are influential in a given community to both help solicit investors, as well as buffer you from complaints when things go badly.

In conclusion, before launching your crime spree, spend some serious time studying potential victims and calculating the likelihood that they'll come after you. Search for a victim who has more to lose by publicly acknowledging versus concealing, the loss.

Even once you have identified a perfect victim, plan your interactions or dealings in a manner calculated to reduce the probability he or she will ever complain. As a general rule, the more personal the relationship, the more embarrassing the betrayal will be. If you can make the client arguably complicit in the wrongdoing, such as involved in inappropriate solicitations (wining, dining, hookers, blow, or kickbacks), then there's virtually no chance he'll come after you.

Research Potential Victims

There is a perfect victim for every type of crime. Before launching your crime spree, spend some serious time studying potential victims and calculating the likelihood that they'll come after you. Search for a victim who has more to lose by publicly acknowledging versus concealing, the loss.

As a general rule, the more personal the relationship, the more embarrassing the betrayal will be. If you can make the client arguably complicit in the wrongdoing, such as involved in inappropriate solicitations (wining, dining, hookers, blow, or kickbacks), then there's virtually no chance he'll come after you.

9

HOW TO GET PAID HANDSOMELY FOR DOING NOTHING

To most of the sane world, charging clients lots of money for doing nothing—providing no meaningful product or service—sounds like the very definition of fraud. But much of what happens every day on Wall Street is far from rational or fair.

The wonderful news for scammers is that Wall Street has devised perfectly legal ways of getting paid millions for doing nothing. Better still, investors—even the most sophisticated—routinely consent to these outrageously abusive payment agreements. So, scammers should feel free to incorporate into their investor agreements the acceptable, commonplace payment-for-nothing schemes. The two most common are:

- Placement agent fees; and
- Fees on committed, uninvested capital.

Don't get too hung up on the names or workings of these specific well-established practices—you should feel free to creatively conceive your own rip-off arrangement. Just accept that there are means by which you can get paid handsomely for doing nothing. If it can be done, why wouldn't you?

Let's begin with placement agent fees.

In 2012, I was retained as independent counsel to a whistleblower trustee of the Kentucky state pension system, Christopher Tobe, who had reported apparent securities fraud to the SEC. I concluded in a special report to the SEC that $14 million in undisclosed payments had been made in connection with the state's pension investments—millions in kick-backs secretly paid to so-called "placement agents" who provided **little or no actual services** to the pension.

Pension officials and the Kentucky State Auditor disagreed with my expert opinion and, through tortuous reasoning, concluded paying millions to secret "agents"—influence-peddling middlemen—for doing nothing harmed no one. Nobody disputed that the middlemen did nothing to deserve getting paid millions. That much was obvious. Yet nobody wanted to go after the $14 million that had been pilfered—despite the fact that the pension was severely underfunded at that time (and is now reportedly on the verge of bankruptcy).[8] While the SEC investigated the apparent violations I reported, in the end the federal agency took no action.

WHAT IS A "PLACEMENT AGENT"?

A "placement agent" is a dispensable intermediary (i.e. unnecessary middleman) who gets paid a lot of money by Wall Street managers for supposedly assisting in the selling of their investment funds. Often, particularly in the case of large investors the placement agent does nothing at all. That's because these $1 billion+ investors already pay experts (investment consultants) of their own to search for, analyze, and recommend good investments. The last thing these investors want or need is an unknowledgeable middleman pushing a particular investment and undermining the integrity of the impartial expert review of the competitive landscape. A

---

8   Report of Independent Counsel to SEC: Placement Agent Abuses at Kentucky Retirement System.

placement agent can be a small one-person independent firm or as large as a division of a global investment bank.

> To most of the sane world, charging clients lots of money for doing nothing—providing no meaningful product or service—sounds very much like the very definition of fraud. But much of what happens every day on Wall Street is far from rational or fair.

Theoretically, professional placement agents are required to be registered with the securities regulatory agency in their jurisdiction, such as the US Securities and Exchange Commission. A placement agent operating in the US must be registered as a broker or dealer. Nevertheless, many placement agents exposed in the past have not been registered anywhere.

Placement agents claim the services they provide go well beyond merely marketing costly, risky investment products. Some placement agents claim to provide value-added services, such as preparing marketing materials, formulating a targeted marketing strategy, organizing roadshows, and even negotiating fee agreements on behalf of the fund. Ironically, in my forensic investigations I've found that investors often aren't aware of:

1. The existence of the placement agent;
2. Any services the placement agent has supposedly provided; or
3. The millions in fees the placement agent was paid.

New, unproven fund managers depend the most upon third-party placement agents because they can't afford to pay for full-time in-house marketers of their own and because certain placement agents are only useful in particular situations. For example, a placement agent who is cozy with Republican officials may be of no use when marketing to Democratic decision-makers and vice versa. Some placement agents have even more limited influence: Often in a given locality a specific person, such as the brother of the mayor, is known as the go-to person for contracting with the city. Anywhere else in the world, the brother is worthless but *in that particular city*, he's essential to getting hired.

The placement agent is compensated upon the successful sale of the investment to investor(s) introduced by, or otherwise assigned to, the agent. The agent's compensation, around 2% to 3%, is typically a percentage of new money raised for the fund.

In 2014, I clued *Forbes* readers into the middleman or "placement agent" scam:

Forget the old adage, "work smarter, not harder." A decade ago, the savviest Wall Streeters discovered a way to make millions doing no work at all.

You can't "work" any smarter than that in my book.

If the chance to make millions for doing little or nothing is appealing to you, it's not too late to get in on the action. Anyone can become a so-called pension placement agent—no investment experience or education is required.[9]

FEES ON COMMITTED, UNINVESTED CAPITAL

Getting paid fees on "committed, uninvested capital" may sound a bit more intimidating but it's really the same thing: scammers get paid for doing nothing. Since nearly all (90%) of alternative investment funds charge these outrageous fees it is clear investors overwhelming are willing to pay them.[10]

Here's how the scam works: The managers of alternative investment funds hire lawyers to draft binding provisions in their contracts which provide that the investor agrees to pay fees

---

[9] https://www.forbes.com/sites/edwardsiedle/2014/06/25/
     billions-for-bupkis-pension-placement-agents/#21dc39384f11

[10] https://www.pionline.com/article/20170725/INTERACTIVE/
     170729897/fees-on-committed-capital-the-norm-in-private-
     equity-funds

on the total amount of money he commits to invest in a fund over time, regardless of whether the entire amount of money is actually invested.

So, imagine I contractually agree (commit) to invest $1 million (capital) in a fund over the next ten years, but only actually put $100,000 initially into the fund early on. If the fee is 3% annually on committed capital (including the uninvested amount of $900,000), I will be charged fees of 3% annually on $1 million or $30,000, not 3% of $100,000 or $3,000—even though the manager is only actually handling (investing) $100,000 of my money initially.

This makes no sense. Why would you ever pay someone a fee to "manage" portions of your money he never touches? Note that in the above example, 3% on "committed, uninvested capital" equates to an astronomical fee of 30% of the $100,000 actually invested initially.

A 2015 forensic investigation of the Rhode Island state pension I undertook on behalf of the thousands of workers belonging to the American Federation of State, County, and Municipal Employees Council 94 revealed that the pension was paying a group of money managers $30 million a year in fees on money that had yet to be invested—fees to Wall Street for **doing nothing.**

Likewise, my 2016 investigation of the New York State Teamsters Pension on behalf of its 35,000 participants showed the near-collapse pension paid $4.5 million in fees to Wall Street on committed, uninvested assets annually for **nothing.**

It should come as no surprise that reportedly some of the largest, most sophisticated investors recently have begun to question this practice. What is remarkable is that the audacious scam of charging fees on committed, uninvested capital has endured for so long.

Once again, this is great news for scammers. Be bold, be creative, be greedy, and you will be richly rewarded! And, remember, no matter how devious your scam may seem to you, there's probably someone on Wall Street who's already doing it (or something very similar)—legally.

10

DON'T WORRY ABOUT COPS, STEAL FROM THEM!

If you're going to be involved in investment scamming, you need to understand the legal and regulatory structure of the investment advisory or money management industry. You need to know which laws or regulations you can skirt, or break; who, i.e., which agencies may come after you for your bad behavior; and the limitations of different regulators and law enforcement.

A "security" is a broad term that includes many types of investments, such as municipal bonds, corporate stock and bonds, bank notes, investment contracts, and more. Securities fraud occurs when someone involved with one of these investments lies, cheats, or steals in an attempt to gain a financial advantage.

The US Securities and Exchange Commission is an independent agency of the federal government which holds primary responsibility, i.e., jurisdiction, for enforcing the federal securities laws, proposing securities rules, and regulating the securities industry, which is the nation's stock and options exchanges, as well as the money management industry.

The bad news is, if you engage in securities fraud the SEC may come after you.

The SEC can bring a *civil* action in a US District Court, or an administrative proceeding which is heard by an independent administrative law judge. At worst, you will receive a fine, a black mark on your record, and a suspension or ban from the securities industry.

The good news: Most SEC cases end up with out-of-court settlements in which the scammer pays a fine or endures a temporary suspension *without admitting guilt*. Firms and individuals who accept such settlements typically publicly state they did nothing wrong and claim they settled just to get the cases behind them and to save legal costs.

More good news: The SEC does not have *criminal* authority and the fines and penalties it seeks rarely represent more than a fraction, say 10-20%, of the amount stolen. Steal a million, pay a $100,000 fine ten years later when you get caught—long after you bought and enjoyed that ski chalet. Go to Vail, not jail.

However, the SEC may refer cases to state and federal prosecutors, like the Federal Bureau of Investigation, for criminal prosecution. But, if you scam smartly, you needn't lose any sleep over that.

It has often been said the SEC has no teeth and its bark is worse than its bite. Further, the agency has long been accused of being effectively captured by—and subservient to—the industry it is supposed to be objectively regulating. Experts have opined that the SEC is a prime candidate for "regulatory capture" for two reasons:

"First, the lawyers (the majority of SEC professional staff) who work in the regulation writing divisions often find their best, and best by a wide margin, post-SEC employment opportunities working for the regulatees, and must change fields completely if they go elsewhere. Second, the inherent complexity of the institutions of the securities industry and its regulatory apparatus create substantial fixed costs that purveyors of influence must conquer in order to be effective. These two factors make for powerful forces that push the SEC in the direction of rule changes that help rather than hurt the powerful incumbents of the securities industry."[11]

---

[11] Regulatory Capture at the U.S. Securities and Exchange Commission, Prepared for the Milken Institute Conference on Capital Markets, March 16, 1998, Santa Monica, California, Susan E. Woodward.

Revolving door + complexity = regulatory capture.

As a former SEC attorney who has worked with the agency for over three decades, I have witnessed countless examples of the SEC failing to take effective action to combat fraud in the securities industry. Regulatory capture is a reality, which is bad for investors but great for scammers.

In addition to federal regulators and statutes, each state also has its own laws about securities fraud and its own state securities commission. While any securities fraud might be punishable under either state or federal law, such crimes are most often prosecuted as federal crimes. The state securities regulators pay their employees a whole lot less than the SEC and, as a result, their staffs are generally far less knowledgeable. Worry least about the state regulators.

Convicted Hedge Fund Manager Agrees to SEC Industry Bar

September 26, 2019 - The Securities and Exchange Commission today issued an order barring a self-proclaimed New Jersey hedge fund manager, Nicholas Lattanzio, from associating with any broker, dealer, investment adviser, municipal securities dealer, municipal advisor, transfer agent, or nationally recognized statistical rating organization.

The SEC previously charged Lattanzio with committing securities and investment advisory fraud. In its complaint filed in federal court in New Jersey in 2015, the SEC alleged that Lattanzio had defrauded two small companies out of more than $4 million by posing as a hedge fund manager who could arrange project financing for them in exchange for an investment in one of his funds. Lattanzio falsely stated that the fund had as much as $800 million under management and a proven track record of producing double-digit returns. As soon as the investors deposited their money into the fund, Lattanzio used the money to fund lavish personal expenses for himself and his family, including a luxury automobile, expensive jewelry, a home in an affluent neighborhood, and private school tuition.

The US Attorney's Office for the District of New Jersey brought parallel criminal charges against Lattanzio. He was convicted at trial on two counts of securities fraud and two counts of wire fraud, and was sentenced to prison and ordered to pay restitution to the victims of his fraud.

Only a small fraction of all securities fraud cases are handled as criminal cases and even when criminal convictions are obtained, prison sentences for these non-violent, white-collar crimes are not common. SEC civil fines often match or exceed those imposed in criminal cases, so prosecutors feel there is little to gain from the extra effort it takes to bring criminal cases.

A criminal case requires proof beyond a reasonable doubt, while proof in a civil case requires only a preponderance of the evidence. Unlike your typical thief, investment scammers often can afford teams of lawyers, many of whom are former prosecutors or regulators (revolving door guys and gals) skilled at finding the holes in the prosecutors' cases.

3 Hallmarks of High-Level Investment Fraud

- Nobody ever admits guilt.
- Nobody ever goes to jail.
- Nobody ever pays back all the money they have stolen.

Also, securities fraud cases are often extremely complex and difficult to explain to juries. Juries have trouble understanding investment scamming cases and most US attorneys' offices don't have expertise in such matters. The US Attorney in New York City is the only one in the country with a standing securities fraud team.

In my experience, law enforcement—including the FBI, often doesn't understand investment scamming cases and, for this reason, fails to recognize criminal activity or prosecute these cases.

Investment fraud criminal cases which require additional effort to prove guilt BARD, as well as an understanding of complex financial concepts almost never happen. The more complex the fraud, the more difficult to prove criminal intent and the less likely prosecutors and juries will be able to understand. Whether you know it or not, the criminal fraud convictions you read about are the most straightforward and seemingly stupid. It's not that all fraudsters are idiots—the masterminds you never hear of, never get caught.

You may have heard of the KISS principle. KISS is an acronym for "keep it simple, stupid," a design principle supposedly originated by the US Navy in 1960. The KISS principle states that simplicity should be a key goal in design, and unnecessary complexity should be avoided.

In scamming, follow a non-KISS approach: devise intentionally overly-complex schemes—schemes which can even be painstakingly disclosed in your sales materials—but which neither investors nor regulators/law enforcement will be able to understand or prosecute.

> **Non-KISS principle**: Intentionally overly-complex financial schemes are less likely to be prosecuted.

It may be surprising to learn that police and law enforcement officers get defrauded by investment scammers—all the time.

Their great instincts—"radar"—when it comes to spotting seedy criminal activity, involving drug dealers, prostitutes, pimps, and thugs, completely fail them when judging socially prominent, well-educated, well-spoken, well-groomed, white-collar investment con-men. Cops trust, respect, and even envy these seemingly prosperous pillars of the community wholeheartedly. Even law enforcement realizes it's got a problem—that's why I have been asked to talk to FBI agents and others in law enforcement about how to protect themselves from investment scammers.

In my speeches, I like to show cops in the audience two pictures—one of a young man dressed thuggishly and another of a mature stockbroker dressed in a designer suit, starched white dress shirt, and tie.

Who poses a greater threat to your financial well-being, I ask them to consider. Who is more likely to get access to the greatest chunk of your wealth and run with it?

WHO POSES A GREATER RISK
TO YOUR FINANCIAL WELL-BEING?

Below is an example of a smaller scam with police as victims that was busted by the SEC.

In conclusion, I raise this issue not because I seriously want you to target cops for thievery; rather, I want to emphasize that investment scamming falls within a law enforcement blind spot. Law enforcement training and instincts are generally not helpful when it comes to rooting out investment fraud. Further, lack of sophistication in investment matters also makes it difficult for law enforcement to respond appropriately to investment wrong-doing. For example, in the law enforcement mindset, if a criminal misappropriates $5 million from a client but seven years later (promptly, after being confronted regarding the wrongful taking) agrees to repay the money, there is no crime worth prosecuting because the victim has been "made whole." He got all his money back, right?

From an investment perspective, however, with 10% compounding, money doubles every seven years. So, over the seven-year period, the criminal has stolen and the victim has lost $5 million. That's a lot of money—well worth prosecuting, in my opinion.

Bottomline: Law enforcement, including the FBI, often neither "get" nor are effective prosecuting investment scammers. You should neither fear nor, in your search for perfect victims, automatically exclude them.

SEC Charges CEO and Company With Defrauding First Responders and Others Out of Millions

Washington, DC, July 30, 2020

The Securities and Exchange Commission today announced charges against a San Antonio-area businessman and his company for running a multimillion-dollar fraudulent scheme that victimized scores of investors, many of them retired San Antonio police officers and other first responders.

The SEC's complaint alleges that Victor Lee Farias and his company, Integrity Aviation & Leasing (IAL), raised $14 million from investors, promising that they would use the funds to purchase engines and other aircraft parts for leasing to major airlines. As alleged, Farias and IAL falsely touted Farias's supposed investment experience and IAL's purported competitive advantages, such as an algorithm that supposedly identified profitable leasing opportunities, and represented that all investments would be secured by IAL's assets. According to the complaint, many of the investors were retirees who, in order to invest their retirement funds, had to withdraw the funds from their retirement accounts and deposit them in newly created self-directed IRA accounts. The complaint alleges that IAL never purchased any engines and spent only a small portion of investor funds on aircraft parts. Farias and IAL allegedly diverted more than $11.6 million for unauthorized purposes, such as making $6.5 million in Ponzi-like payments to investors and investing $2.7 million to fund a friend's business. Farias also allegedly misappropriated $2.4 million for personal expenses. According to the complaint, Farias continued to mislead investors after he learned of the SEC's investigation, including by using the letterhead from the SEC's investigative subpoena as "proof" for investors that he was working with the SEC to take IAL public.

11

HOW SCAMMERS DEFINE SUCCESS

A t the outset of any endeavor, it is helpful to define the goal, or what constitutes "success."

A "successful" investment professional, or scammer, makes money, first and foremost, for *himself.* Whether the investment services he provides for the exorbitant fee he charges are crappy, competitive, or superior, few will ever truly know. Even the clients themselves will be largely clueless due to the complexities and ambiguities of evaluating investments. Most clients are incapable of judging investment performance and can be persuaded bad performance is, in fact, good. We'll talk more later about how to explain-away bad performance results.

If a money manager makes millions or billions for himself, all will agree he's a "success." They will ask no further questions—such as whether he's really a successful *investor.*

> If a money manager makes millions or billions for himself, all will agree he's a "success."

Most of the best-known money managers have actually lost more money than they ever made for clients. In part, that's because investors tend to throw money at celebrated managers enjoying a winning streak—assets under management peaking just before the manager's luck runs out. So when the manager's performance inevitably reverts to the mean, or long-run average, more money is lost than was made over the run-up because there is more money under his management to lose.

While sticking investors with egregious fees for bar tabs and private jets, on top of the lavish asset-based and performance fees they charge, might seem overly ambitious for financial advisers, such gouging is common on Wall Street and acceptable to regulators and investors.

For example, according to Reuters:

Millennium, the $34 billion New York firm led by billionaire Israel Englander, charged clients its usual fees of 5 or 6 percent of assets and 20 percent of gains in 2016, according to a person familiar with the situation. The charges left investors in Millennium's flagship fund with a net return of just 3.3 percent.

Citadel, the $26 billion Chicago firm led by billionaire Kenneth Griffin, charged pass-through fees that added up to about 5.3 percent in 2015 and 6.3 percent in 2014, according to another person familiar with the situation. Charges for 2016 were not finalized, but the costs typically add up to between 5 and 10 percent of assets, separate from the 20 percent performance fee Citadel typically charges.

Citadel's flagship fund returned 5 percent in 2016, far below its 19.5 percent annual average since 1990, according to the source who, like others, spoke on the condition of anonymity because the information is private.[12]

So, be brutally honest with yourself (and only yourself): Are you interested in managing the wealth of others to make these fat cats even wealthier and get a grateful pat on the back, or to surreptitiously transfer as much of that wealth to yourself as possible? At some point in their careers most money managers cross that bridge, or line, and decide that their primary goal is

---

[12] http://www.reuters.com/article/us-hedgefunds-passthrough-insigh t-idUSKBN1530JL

to maximize their personal wealth, i.e., get rich at the expense of their clients.

The sooner you define your goal, the more efficient you will be in pursuing it and the sooner you'll achieve it.

Selfless or selfish, bait or shark, the choice is yours.

To be sure, making your client's money grow—showing positive investment returns—is good for business. And in a strong, rising market, you should be able to easily skim some of those gains from client accounts while leaving them with enough so that they don't notice or complain.

When the stock market is up 15%, investors who net 10% are thrilled. But, as Buffett once famously said, "Only when the tide goes out do you discover who's been swimming naked." In other words, you don't really know or appreciate the skills of an investment adviser until they are tested by adverse conditions. It's easy to look like a genius in a bull market.

When the market stumbles or plummets, it's not quite so easy to continue gouging clients. It can be done but you'll have to employ additional devices we'll discuss later, like inflating portfolio values and using inappropriate benchmark comparisons, to keep clients in the dark and happy.

12

YOU <u>WILL</u> NEED SELLING DOCUMENTS

To repeat, if you want to steal a lot of money and not get prosecuted, you've got to convince people to *willingly* hand their money over to you. No thuggery allowed.

When peddling investments, you will need to provide prospective investors with marketing materials, contracts to manage their money and to purchase shares of your investment fund, as well as other selling documents. The most formal of these documents is the "offering memorandum" or "private placement memorandum." These documents should be as professionally written and persuasive as any selling materials created by big Wall Street firms. Your documents must portray a valuable investment that anyone should feel fortunate to have the opportunity to invest in. The "opportunity of a lifetime."

You want to impress investors with your knowledge of the industry you're involved in and insights/advantages that will enable you to crush the competition. There's no excuse for typos, or sloppy wording.

Templates of all of these forms of materials are readily (and cheaply) available today online, as are many such documents in actual use by Wall Street participants.

Nevertheless, this is not the place to skimp. Whatever you spend on selling documents is an investment in your future success.

If you're not a great writer—and chances are, you're not—hire someone who is. As I learned years ago writing for *Forbes,* a great editor will make you look vastly smarter. On the other hand, poorly drafted marketing, contract, and deal documents are a dead giveaway that you're either not serious or an idiot. If you can't even put together convincing sales materials in the internet age, why should anyone give you their money?

But there is a far more compelling reason to painstakingly prepare these documents—even though few investors will actually read them.

Despite the legal fiction that contracts are written agreements freely entered into, fairly negotiated between parties of equal strength with equal access to information, that's pure bullshit—as you know from everyday life. Consumer contracts are almost never negotiated or substantially modified by the customer, or investor. Ever tried negotiating the terms of your contract with a cell phone or car rental company or airline? Good luck with that!

The truth is, he who writes the agreement largely defines its final terms. Even if the consumer wanted to modify the investment contract and the company agreed to allow him to freely do so, he almost certainly would not possess knowledge equal to or greater than the Wall Street firm that wrote the contract. This is referred to as "asymmetric information" which occurs when one party to an economic transaction possesses greater material knowledge than the other party. In complex investment matters, the asymmetry is profound. Even if the investor was provided with full access to all the relevant information—which never happens—he still wouldn't be able to make sense of it. A fairly sophisticated understanding of the management of money, as well as industry practices and regulation is required. (And investors that possess such in-depth knowledge probably wouldn't be hiring a Wall Street flunky to manage their wealth.)

So, seize the opportunity to insert into the contracts and agreements you pay someone else to draft for you every type of unfair provision you ever dreamed of—e.g., fees on committed, uninvested capital; limitations of liability; mandatory arbitration provisions; and limits on redemptions—all of which are commonplace and which investors, like sheep, routinely accept.

In your selling materials, you are required by federal and state regulators to include certain information which supposedly provides protection for the investor. But overwhelmingly your sales materials—like all of Wall Street's—will favor and protect you. So take the time to write them right.

Seize the opportunity to insert into the agreements you pay someone to draft for you every type of unfair provision you ever dreamed of.

Overwhelmingly your sales materials—like all of Wall Street's—will favor and protect you.

As mentioned above, the lengthiest sales document you may have to prepare is the offering memorandum. The typical offering memorandum contents include:

1. Summary of the Offering
2. Business Summary
3. Requirements for Purchasers
4. Forward-Looking Information (Financial)
5. Risk Factors
6. Use of Proceeds
7. Management
8. Compensation
9. Board of Directors
10. Capitalization Table and Dilution
11. Legal Information

The goal of an offering document is to give investors a detailed explanation about the nature of the investment; the strategy and objective; how the investments will be managed and by whom. You'll want to highlight, i.e., inflate, your past successes and project impressive future results.

Included with the Offering Memorandum you may hand out to investors is a "Subscription Agreement," generally at the end of the document or in its appendices. The Subscription Agreement establishes the terms under which the subscriber is purchasing shares in your scheme. The investor is required to represent or warrant that she:

1. Has received all the relevant materials and understands them;

2. Meets the suitability and eligibility requirements;

3. Has sufficient knowledge and experience in financial matters so as to be capable of evaluating and bearing the risks of the investment, including a complete loss;

4. Agrees to indemnify and hold harmless the fund against virtually any claim of wrongdoing;

5. Agrees to waive his right to go to court, including the right to a jury trial if a dispute arises.

As the above list amply demonstrates, the Subscription Agreement is all about protecting you and screwing your investors.

In all the materials you hand out to investors, be as upfront as possible about the potential risks (in language no one can understand) to protect yourself against future claims.

After decades of experience, I am convinced that there is no deal so foul a skilled wordsmith cannot make sellable.

The key to selling shit is to make it look and smell like a rose. If your offering documents emphasize a fantastic outcome and capture the investor's imagination or greed, many investors will focus solely on the pot of gold at the end of the rainbow.

They'll overlook any onerous risk disclosure—disclosure which will protect your ass legally.

As mentioned below, there have been selling documents which literally state "I may steal your money." If disclosing you might steal all the investors' money doesn't queer the deal, what will? No disclosure, if properly worded, will deter true believers—if the Kool-Aid is sweet enough.

If the investor is overwhelmed by the beauty of the rose, he'll overlook the thorns.

> There is no deal so foul a skilled wordsmith cannot make sellable.
>
> The key to selling shit is to make it look and smell like a rose.

13

DIRTY ROTTEN SCOUNDREL DISCLOSURE

Financial advisors are generally required under the federal securities laws to disclose all important or what regulators call "material" information to investors. Disclosures can be negative or positive in nature but generally the more you disclose the negatives, the less likely you'll be sued when the crappy investment you've sold to investors fails to perform well *for them*—even as it adds to your bottomline.

Fortunately for scammers, disclosure statements are always written by lawyers to protect the sellers of the bogus products and are intentionally worded to be incomprehensible to the average reader. Lawyers use "boilerplate" clauses that are verbose and written in awkward legalese. Disclosures are often printed in small type (aka "micro-print") because they are so lengthy, which makes it all-the-more likely they will never be read by the investor. In short, industry-wide practices and disclosures are so reprehensible that candid awful disclosures by scammers—hucksters focused exclusively upon abusing clients—can be indistinguishable from industry norms. Just say and do what the big Wall Street firms say and do. Do not hesitate to disclose what a dirty rotten scoundrel you are. No alarms will go off in investors' minds.

Industry-wide practices and disclosures are so reprehensible that candid awful disclosures by scammers—hucksters focused exclusively upon abusing clients—can be indistinguishable from industry norms. Just say and do what the big Wall Street firms say and do.

As hard as it may be to believe, getting investors to consent to outrageous behavior that is harmful to them, including even criminal acts such as theft, is easy. The highest-paid firms, managing hedge and private equity funds, do it all the time. For example, the Madoff feeder funds disclosed that there was a risk "the broker may abscond with the assets." When the Madoff funds finally got caught, they defended saying, "We disclosed we might steal all the money—you agreed to the potential theft and, so, have no reason to complain. We did exactly what we told you we might do." For decades this alarming disclosure did not hinder Madoff from raking in and pilfering billions.

I recommend getting a skilled lawyer to assist with the disclosure task but here are some pointers.

To accomplish the consent to outrageous behavior, even thievery, objective:

- Disclose "potential," not actual wrongdoing. Always refer to "potential" outcomes that "may" happen—even though you know damn well (from the get-go) they *will*.

  The words, "We may charge unauthorized fees from time to time…" means—and you know this—we ABSOLUTELY WILL! No business ever discloses it may screw you without fully intending to do so.

- Characterize disastrous possible outcomes as benign (matter-of-fact without pejoratives); keep the language as impersonal and incomprehensible as possible. Term obvious wrongdoing as "conflicts" and "risks."

For example, "I will kill you" in legal-speak disclosure becomes:

"There is the potential risk that the adviser or parties affiliated with the adviser may engage in certain actions which could impact investor longevity or contravene applicable law, if subject to scrutiny by law enforcement."

- Get the client to agree to be kept in the dark (i.e., consent to the withholding of damning information) as much as possible. If you can talk the client into agreeing that you do not have to provide important negative information which should be disclosed under the law, then you're free to engage in nastiness.
- Last and equally important, is the client promise of secrecy. Get the investor to agree to keep the bad stuff you disclose about yourself secret from other investors and, of course, regulators and law enforcement.

The last two items amount to getting the client to believe you and he are both on the same side. What's good for you is good for him. Get the client to agree to be complicit in the very scheme that screws him.

> Get the client to agree to be complicit in the very scheme that screws him.
> Consent + Secrecy = Complicity.

The accomplished shyster gets his victims to guzzle so much of the magic Kool-Aid that they recite his bogus representations in his defense long after the money's gone—because that's preferable to acknowledging they got duped and are, in part, to blame.

Convince the client that outrageous wrongdoing is acceptable—no cause for concern.

Soothingly tell the clients that secrecy is necessary for the investment magic—the alchemy—to work and is, therefore, in his best interest.

"If I disclose the unique opportunities I'm pursuing in your portfolio, then the whole world would know about them—snap them up—and there'd be nothing left for you. You need—we need—secrecy for this whole investment strategy to work."

My forensic investigations in Rhode Island and North Carolina detailed how these massive, multi-billion-dollar taxpayer-funded state pensions consented to wrongdoing and promised Wall Street secrecy.

As I wrote in my $8 billion Rhode Island pension report:

"The willingness of Rhode Island pension officials and others (such as the Governor, Attorney General and Auditor General) to agree to an unprecedented secrecy scheme proposed by Wall Street that effectively eviscerates the state Access to Public Records Act, today fosters potential pilfering from the pension and lawlessness—such as charging bogus fees, tax fraud, insider trading, front-running, and engaging in self-dealing.

Wrongdoers are not held accountable, rather are shielded from public scrutiny."[13]

Secrecy at the $85 billion North Carolina pension is costing state taxpayers billions more, I wrote:

"The profound lack of transparency related to these risky so-called "alternative" investments provides investment managers ample opportunities to charge excessive fees, carry out transactions on behalf of the pension on unfavorable terms, misuse assets, or even steal them outright. Worse still, the Treasurer has betrayed her fiduciary duty by entering into expansive agreements with Wall Street to keep the very details of their abuse of pension

---

[13]   http://files.golocalprov.com.s3.amazonaws.com/Double%20
Trouble%20FINAL.pdf

assets secret—including withholding information regarding grave potential violations of law.

Kickbacks, self-dealing, fraud, tax evasion, and outright theft may be designated as confidential pursuant to the North Carolina Trade Secrets Protection Act, says the Treasurer.

On a more granular level, Treasurer Cowell's efforts to thwart disclosure have helped mask potential violations including, but not limited to the following: fraudulent representations related to the performance of alternative investments; concealment and intentional understatement of $400 million in annual alternative investment fees and expenses to date; concealment of approximately $180 million in placement agent compensation; the charging of bogus private equity fees; violations of securities broker-dealer registration requirements related to private equity transaction fees; securities and tax law violations regarding investment management fee waivers and monitoring fees; self-dealing involving alternative investment managers; mystery investor liquidity and information preferences, amounting to licenses to steal from TSERS; pension investment consultant conflicts of interest; predatory lending and life settlement related fraud.

Absent reform, corruption of TSERS is likely to cost the state's public workers and taxpayers billions more over the next few years and leave in place a system under which Cowell's successors will compound the financial damage.

Today, TSERS assets are directly invested in approximately 300 funds and indirectly in hundreds more underlying funds (through fund of funds), the names, investment practices, portfolio holdings, investment performances, fees, expenses, regulation, trading, and custodian banking arrangements of which are largely unknown to stakeholders, the State Auditor and, indeed, to even the Treasurer and her staff.

As a result of the lack of transparency and accountability at TSERS, it is virtually impossible for stakeholders to know the answers to questions as fundamental as who is managing the money, what is it invested in, and where is it?"[14]

Over the past decade, some of Wall Street's wealthiest money managers have been busily perfecting new schemes to profit at the expense of their clients.

New gently-worded (so as not to raise alarm) language has been creeping into the investment contracts, offering memorandum, and subscription agreements managers ask investors to sign to the effect that the investor understands and agrees managers may engage in outrageously bad behavior, including criminal acts, as well as keeping the very best investment opportunities for themselves and only passing along the crap deals to their clients.

The litany of potential abusive practices included in the latest iteration of investor disclosure documents and regulatory filings with the SEC should cause investors to scream bloody murder.

That's not happening.

Even so-called "sophisticated" institutions have consented to the newest abuses because they have been assured the dangers vaguely disclosed are more hypothetical than real. Of course, political donations and marketing dollars have greased the way.

You can learn a lot from private equity money managers in particular, about how to disclose the worst possible behavior in a manner clients will not protest and even get clients to consent to your withholding information about your misdeeds—from them.

Let's study some of the real language used in their SEC filings. For example:

"The Adviser and certain employees and affiliates of the Adviser **may** invest in and alongside the Funds, either through the General Partners, as direct investors in the Funds or otherwise... The Adviser and its related entities **may** engage in a broad range of activities, including investment activities for their own

---

[14] https://www.seanc.org/assets/SEANC_Pension_Investigation_Highlights__Recommendations.pdf
https://www.seanc.org/assets/North-Carolina-Report.pdf

account… The Adviser **may**, from time to time, establish certain investment vehicles through which employees of the Adviser and their family members, certain business associates, other "friends of the firm" or other persons **may** invest alongside one or more of the Funds."

"In certain cases, the Adviser **may** cause a Fund to purchase investments from another Fund, or it **may** cause a Fund to sell investments to another Fund (emphasis added throughout)."

Lots of worrisome "mays" in the language above.

Got the drift of what's being said?

Of course not! To understand the range of potential harm to investors from the schemes detailed in the above language would take a lifetime—as well as access to information about financial transactions that have actually happened, as opposed to what "might." And investors are never going to get access to that incriminating information.

Translation from legal-speak: the manager of the investment fund and his friends may directly, or through a special "friends and family" separate investment fund, buy—at a lower cost—shares of the very same company the money manager purchases—at a higher cost—for funds in which clients, i.e., suckers like you, invest. The especially-entitled friends and family fund could profit by holding those lower-cost company shares, or immediately flipping them—selling the shares to funds in which clients--idiots like you--invested at a guaranteed, riskless mark-up amounting to millions.

That's called "front-running"—which is generally illegal—unless the client consents.[15]

Alternatively, the friends and family fund can create and sell start-up companies it owns to funds the investment firm manages for other clients at inflated (above market) prices:

"In addition, the Adviser **may**, from time to time, fund start-up expenses for a portfolio company and **may** subsequently sell such portfolio company to a Fund. Such transactions **may**

---

[15]   https://www.investopedia.com/terms/f/frontrunning.asp

create conflicts of interest because, *by not exposing such buy and sell transactions to market forces,* a Fund **may** not receive the best price otherwise possible, or the Adviser **might** have an incentive to improve the performance of one Fund by selling underperforming assets to another Fund in order, for example, to earn fees (emphasis added)."

That's called "self-dealing"—which is generally illegal—unless the client consents. Why would you ever agree to let someone sell something you own for less than it's worth in the marketplace? And a private sale of your property to a friend of his is almost certainly going to be for less than full value.

In short, whenever someone says others who are "friends and family" may be getting a better deal than you, he's telling you: **you are not his friend and he is not your friend**. That should make you feel like shit.

> Whenever someone says others who are "friends and family" may be getting a better deal than you, he's telling you: **you are not his friend and he is not your friend**.
>
> That should make you feel like shit.

A hedge or private equity firm may also demand investors agree that certain "special" (as opposed to friends and family) investors will be permitted to profit at the expense of other, let's call them "not-so-special" investors.

"The General Partners and/or the Funds may enter into other written agreements ("Side Letters") with one or more limited partners of the Funds. These Side Letters may entitle a limited partner to make an investment in a Fund *on terms other than those described in such Fund's organizational documents.* Any such terms may be *more favorable* than those offered to any other limited partners (emphasis added)."

Screw investors—like me—while you favor other investors whose identity I'll never know? How fair is that? How stupid would I have to be to ever agree to such unequal treatment?

The largest pensions in the nation and wealthiest individuals agree to these unequal treatment provisions all the time—often because they've been assured by Wall Street that *they* are the special investors who will get treated preferentially. The trouble is, once you agree that secret preferential dealings are permissible, you can never be sure you're getting the best deal. It's kinda like your married lover telling you, "You're the only one I've ever cheated with." Do you really know?

I've never seen a private equity offering document that didn't include provisions detailing more favorable treatment for special unnamed investors.

Then there's the luxury private equity managers enjoy of charging investors additional fees, on top of the already hefty asset management and performance fees they charge.

"The Adviser generally may, in its discretion, contract with any related person of the Adviser (including but not limited to a portfolio company of a Fund) to perform services for the Adviser, including in connection with its provision of services to the Funds. In such instances the Funds may bear the cost of such services. When engaging a related person to provide such services, there is a risk that the Adviser may have an incentive to engage the related person *even if another person may be more qualified to provide the applicable services and/or can provide such services at a lesser cost (emphasis added)*."

So, how exactly would the adviser hiring his relations to do something they are *less* qualified to do for *more* money than it would normally cost, be good for you? Why would any rational investor ever agree to this bullshit? Again, chances are the investors never read the disclosure and, if they did, they never understood what it meant.

According to a recent internal review by the SEC, a majority of private-equity firms inflate fees and expenses charged to companies in which they hold stakes. More than half of about 400 private-equity firms that SEC staff examined charged unjustified fees and expenses without notifying investors, said the SEC.[16]

"Transactions fees charged by private equity funds, sometimes called the "crack cocaine of the private equity industry" because the fees are not traditionally subject to minimum performance requirements, are increasingly opposed by large pensions and have recently been the subject of an SEC whistleblower complaint filed by a senior private equity insider. A few years ago Blackstone, the world's largest buyout firm, announced it would end this controversial fee practice that was under scrutiny from regulators and investors."[17]

Insiders secretly profiting "from time to time" at the expense of investors through myriad arrangements is more than a mere possibility—it is a risk most private equity managers obliquely disclose to investors.

Given all of the above disclosed potential conflict of interest and self-dealing scenarios, it should come as no surprise when private equity insiders end up doing a whole lot better than their clients who, at best, have only a whiff of the rank secret dealings.

Better still (for scammers), in recent years private equity crooks have devised new seemingly air-tight agreements which allow them to keep investors in the dark about even *criminal* dealings.

The legalese in SEC filings looks like this:

"The organizational documents of certain Funds permit the Adviser and/or each such Fund's General Partner to **withhold information** from certain limited partners or investors in such Fund in certain circumstances. For instance, information may be withheld from limited partners that are subject to **Freedom of Information Act** or similar requirements. The Adviser and/ or General Partner may elect to **withhold** certain information from such limited partners for reasons relating to the Adviser's

---

16 https://www.bloomberg.com/news/articles/2014-04-07/bogus-private-equity-fees-said-found-at-200-firms-by-sec

17 https://www.wsj.com/articles/blackstone-to-curb-controversial-fee-practice-1412714245

and/or General Partner's **public reputation** or overall business strategy, **despite the potential benefits to such limited partners of receiving such information.** In addition, due to the fact that potential investors in a Fund may ask different questions and request different information, **the Adviser may provide certain information to one or more prospective investors that it does not provide to all prospective investors** (emphasis added throughout)."

In other words, it is possible *and perfectly legal*, in your offering memorandum or other organizational documents, to require investors to consent that if you engage in criminal activity which, if disclosed to them, might make them feel compelled to report the crimes to law enforcement or regulators, or such disclosure would negatively impact your public reputation (not to mention send you to jail), then you may withhold the incriminating information regarding your crimes from them.

If you're thinking no sane client would ever agree to such insanity, you're wrong.

Included among the limited partners that routinely agree to the withholding of incriminating information are state and local government pensions which are subject to state Freedom of Information Act-type laws. State and local pensions are supposed to be subject to public scrutiny because public, i.e., taxpayer and government worker, money is involved.

Study the final sentence in the above disclosure. How can the private equity managers provide material investment information to certain investors and withhold it from others without harming the latter? They can't, in my opinion. Even the managers themselves acknowledge there are "potential benefits to such limited partners of receiving such information."

Withholding a benefit from someone amounts to a detriment, in my book.

Why would thousands of state and local pensions around the nation agree to such obviously unfair treatment by the money managers they hire? If I were a stakeholder—taxpayer or state worker—in one of these funds, I'd want to know.

In conclusion, scammers should get their filthy paws on as many hedge and private equity offering documents as they can and study the sections on conflicts of interest and risk disclosure word-for-word.

A review of the SEC filings of these firms for outrageous disclosures should be reassuring to scammers. There is absolutely nothing worse you can do to abuse clients that the guys on Wall Street haven't already done/disclosed/gotten away with—legally.

That is, there **never** is any excuse for a scammer to conceal any potential bad behavior from victims.

Why would you? There is no such thing as disclosure so bad that it will kill a sale.

So, if you're a scammer, disclose your very worst behavior and be confident that no one will read, comprehend, or be deterred from giving you their money—as long as you choose your words carefully.

There is **never** any excuse for a scammer to conceal potential wrongdoing from victims. There is absolutely nothing worse you can do to abuse clients that the guys on Wall Street haven't already done/disclosed/gotten away with—legally.

Do not hesitate to disclose the dirty rotten scoundrel you are.

14

BEHIND EVERY SUCCESSFUL SCAMMER STANDS A CROOKED LAWYER (AND ACCOUNTANT)

Once upon a time it was said that behind every successful man stood a woman (and behind her, his wife). Likewise, behind every successful investment scammer stands a good lawyer or law firm.

I strongly recommend you seek out an ethically untethered lawyer with proven expertise in facilitating major league Wall Street thievery. Why are lawyers so important and how can you find them?

Have you ever heard the phrase "white shoe Wall Street law firms"? These are law firms, generally based in New York, Boston, Washington, DC, and Chicago which represent the leading investment banking, mutual fund, and money management firms. "White shoe" derives from white bucks, laced suede, or buckskin shoes with a red sole, popular back in the day at Ivy League colleges. My father wore them eighty years ago. I have a pair but they're not so popular these days.

Anyway, young lawyers at these firms work ungodly hours putting investment deals together for the leading global financial firms.

Having an experienced investment-savvy lawyer at your beckon call can reduce the risk you'll get in trouble engaging in the criminality you have in mind. Better still, she can advise you how to modify your scheme to more closely resemble Wall Street scams that have successfully evaded prosecution. Remember that since almost any outrageous investment con can be accomplished legally, why wouldn't you do your scamming legally?

Plus, the big white shoe firms can play an important marketing role. Most investors believe that if you've got a prestigious law firm associated with your deal, it's likely to be legit. The law firms are fully aware of that investor perception and cite the value of their reputations in "capital-raising" when defending their outrageous fees to clients. But when shit hits the fan, they're the first to say that they knew nothing of and played no role in the scam.

So what do start-up scammers who can't afford big-firm prices and aren't located near New York or Boston do?

Look for a lawyer who has spent five or six years at a big firm—someone who's been around Wall Street long enough to have acquired the skills and learned the game—but who was passed over for partnership and forced to go out on his/her own. These guys and gals are a whole lot cheaper and have all the technical skills you will likely need in your early ventures until you score really big.

An intelligent thief masters the rules of the game and the standards he will be judged against. Lawyers can teach you the rules, how to use them to your benefit, and how to work around them.

The more you can recite the rules—the more credible and persuasive you'll be in pitching your rip-off. Smear the rules all over your body for the world to see and to protect you like sunscreen.

You want to have the look and feel of a saintly, trusted advisor, even as you devilishly structure the entire relationship with the client to your exclusive benefit. To smoothly pull off this sleight of hand, you'll need a skilled legal magician. Don't be afraid of lawyers, instead embrace them and use them to your advantage.

Likewise, to "massage" the numbers and assist in capital raising a crooked accountant may be necessary. Chances are, early on, you won't be able to afford one of the Big-Four accounting firms. The good news is you don't need them. As the Madoff case proved, even the most sophisticated investors rarely care about the stature of the accountant. One accountant is as good or bad as the next, they figure.

Scammers Don't Need Big-Four Accountants

Madoff"s auditor of record was a two-person accounting firm based in suburban Rockland County, New York, that had only one active accountant, a close Madoff family friend. The accountant was also an investor in Madoff›s fund, which was later seen as a blatant conflict of interest. Further, major firms all gave clean bills of health to the numerous funds that invested with Madoff. Clients said the large accounting firms signed off on statements that indicated the Madoff investment vehicles had billions of dollars in assets as well as an unlikely track record showing years of always-positive returns.

Also, even if you could get a Big-Four firm on board, you probably don't want a major accounting firm looking over your shoulders until you're more seasoned. Keep in mind, sophisticated accounting clients with established businesses *tell* their accountants what to include, exclude, and say in the financial statements. They know they can structure their relationships with their accountants in a manner which is both consistent with their business goals and comfortable for the squeamish bean-counters. Wall Streeters are notorious for persuading their accountants to say whatever's needed to make the sale.

It is helpful to keep in mind what audit reports really say. The standard report says in the opening paragraph that the firm did an audit but that the financial statements are the responsibility of management. The responsibility for financial statement presentation lies squarely in the hands of the company being audited. The firm merely expresses an opinion on them. In the next paragraph the firm states that it carried out audit procedures that provided a reasonable basis for expressing an opinion, but the firm did not necessarily catch everything. Contrary to commonly-held beliefs, standard audits do *not* look for fraud. The primary responsibility for the prevention and detection of fraud rests with those managing the fund. To detect fraud, forensic investigations or a "fraud audit" is generally required. Finally, the firm states that in its opinion, the company's financial statements conform to accounting and financial reporting standards and are not misleading. In short, a clean audit offers no guarantee that a fund's accounting is completely above board.

Limiting the scope of your audit, whereby the auditor is instructed by you not to perform any auditing procedures with respect to certain investment information is an example of a means of structuring your relationship with an accountant to ensure he doesn't have a clue about your scamming.

So, before engaging an accountant for your scam, don't be intimidated. You're in the driver's seat. Shop for an accountant who is malleable—willing to go along with your scam and structure your relationship to ensure he's kept in the dark.

An intelligent thief masters the rules of the game and the standards he will be judged against. Lawyers can teach you the rules, how to use them to your benefit, and how to work around them. Smear the rules all over your body for the world to see and to protect you like sunscreen.

Sophisticated accounting clients with established businesses *tell* their accountants what to include, exclude, and say in the financial statements. Shop for an accountant who is malleable—willing to go along with your scam and structure your relationship to ensure he's kept in the dark.

15

THE ELEGANCE OF WEALTH
TRANSFER SCHEMES

Now, let's get back to my bastardization of the Kipling poem, *If*, at the opening of this book.

If—
If you can devise a scheme,
Built upon foolish dreams;
That transfers wealth of others to you,
Dollar-for-dollar—patiently over time,
Without conviction of any crime;
You'll never go hungry...

Let me explain the elegant mathematics of a "wealth transfer" scheme to you in the simplest way possible.

Imagine you create an investment fund and persuade someone to invest $1 million. Your fund charges an industry standard one-time, up-front placement fee or commission of 3% and each year charges fees of 7% for ongoing management of the investments—a recurring fee which is high, but not unheard of. Each year you take the commissions and fees the investor pays you and invest them in an account of your own. Assume both the fund you manage for clients and the money you earn from it deposited in your private account grow at the same rate of 10% per year.

Next we add-in compound interest which Albert Einstein supposedly called the "Eighth wonder of the world" and about which he supposedly said, "He who understands it, earns it; he who doesn't, pays it." Compound interest is the interest you'll earn on your interest reinvested.

Thanks to compound interest, in eight years you'll have an amount *in your pocket* equal to that $1 million the investor entrusted to you. Simple enough, right?

That's perfectly legal.

So the lesson here is:

Clueless crooks who grab $1 million—go to jail.

Savvy swindlers who calculatedly skim $1 million over time— go to Vail.

Jail or Vail—you choose.

In other words, you can kill the cow and briefly gorge on steak (and then go swiftly to jail) or milk it for nearly a lifetime.

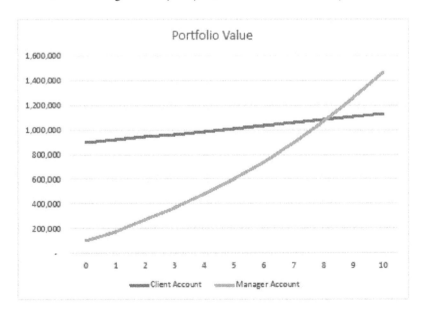

But there's a lot more to the math of stealing smartly.

If you include additional hidden expenses and charges; if you inflate the value of the assets upon which your annual fee is based, you can effectuate the wealth transfer in an even shorter period of time—perhaps five years.

On the other hand, the greater the number of years—the longer you stretch out your thievery—the lower the percentage skimmed each year has to be for you to end up with as much money as your client and the less likely your client will complain or even notice the skimming.

Best of all, even after the $1 million, eight-year wealth transfer, money skimmed from the client's funds keeps flowing to you—perhaps for as long as fifty years (as we'll discuss later).

As the chart below indicates, after twenty years, you'll have made over $5 million off your client's $1 million investment and he'll be left with a paltry $1.4 million. You have used his money to make yourself rich—legally. And that's how we define success in the investment industry: you made money. How the client fares is a secondary concern, at best.

So my disciple Duncan—remember Duncan?—after successfully raising $10 million from investors he could, twenty years from now, end up fabulously wealthy with $50 million in his pocket—having used his clients' money to make himself far richer than any of them.

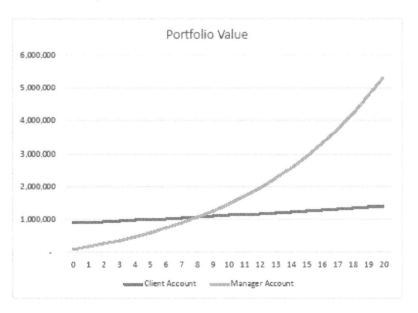

Of course, the more client money invested in your fund, the faster you—like many uber-wealthy Wall Streeters—will become at least as rich as any single client.

And you don't have to gouge investors with fees as high as 7%. Indeed, skimming even one-tenth of 1% off hundreds of millions or billions in client assets like Wall Street does will result in you becoming significantly—exponentially—wealthier than any of your trusting investors.

So, what kind of an investment charges clients fees of 7% or more? You may be aware that traditional investments, such as mutual funds, charge fees more like 1-1.5%.

But in recent years Wall Street has moved on to far greener pastures. Only chumps are peddling mutual funds that charge a paltry 1%, or less, in fees nowadays.

Remember the 1967 film, *The Graduate* when Ben, a recent college graduate who is talented but aimless, is given employment advice by his dad's friend Mr. McGuire?

"I want to say two words to you. Just two words."

"Yes," said Ben.

"Are you listening?"

"Yes, I am," said Ben.

But instead of "plastics," I'm saying, "hedge and private equity funds."

If you want to make big money these days, you need to study hedge and private equity funds. Better still, hedge and private equity *fund of funds* which have fees on top of fees. Or *funds of funds of funds* (yes, they really do exist) which have three layers of onerous fees. These investments so badly rip-off clients with mind-blowing fees that there's no way they'll ever come out ahead of the game—actually see any meaningful return on their money. On the other hand, the scammers packaging and promoting them can't lose.

Most firms offering these costly hedge and private equity fund of funds do not disclose the overall fees to investors. In fact, they go to great lengths to hide the costs and mislead investors. However, here's the most straightforward disclosure of onerous fees I've ever seen from a hedge fund of funds, which proves that outrageous fee disclosures do not prevent a scammer from raising BILLIONS.

SHAREHOLDER TRANSACTION FEES

Maximum sale load (percentage of offering price)	3%
Maximum repurchase fee	None

ANNUAL EXPENSES

Advisory fee	1.50%
Interest payments on borrowed funds	0.02%
Other expenses	0.37%
Acquired fund fees and expenses	4.18%
Total Annual Expenses	6.07%

A forensic investigation of the fees and expenses of even the fund detailed above would almost certainly reveal additional transactional fees (brokerage commissions) of 1-3%, based upon my experience.

In short, study the most elegant wealth transfer scheme du jour. There's no need to reinvent the wheel—sell the highest fee investment that suckers are lining up to buy.

The key to success on Wall Street is to structure an offering—an investment product—so you cannot lose and the investors' wealth gradually transfers to you.

Once you've built your Weapon of Mass Financial Destruction, the emphasis shifts to getting it sold—distribution and marketing. The higher the fees and commissions embedded in a financial product—the greater the pot of money available to you for the marketing effort—the more motivated salesmen will be to sell it and the better it will sell.

Perhaps the best-known example of a terrible investment product that pays outrageous commissions to salesmen and sells like hotcakes is the variable annuity. Here's a "simple" explanation of a variable annuity:

A variable annuity is a tax-deferred retirement vehicle that allows you to choose from a selection of costly investment options, and then pays you a level of income in retirement that is determined by the performance of the investments you choose, after deducting multiple applicable fees and expenses.

These costly products are "sold, not bought." That is, highly incentivized salesmen push variable annuities on investors who don't have a clue about the fees and expenses they're paying. No purchaser of a variable annuity has ever understood these investments. If investors understood, they'd never buy this shit.

16

MOST VICTIMS OF FRAUD WON'T SUE

It's often said we're a nation of whiney consumers and that unlucky investors are all-too-quick to file lawsuits. Don't believe it for a second.

In my professional experience, more-often-than-not investors who have been defrauded:

1. Aren't aware they've been fleeced;
2. Don't want to believe they've been victimized by someone they trusted to handle their money;
3. Don't want to get involved in an ugly investigation of potential wrongdoing; and
4. Feel powerless to bring a successful lawsuit and recover their monies, so why bother?

Even when the largest, supposedly most "sophisticated" investors get swindled out of millions or billions, ironically the level of sophistication required to grapple with the fraud is almost always lacking. It's complex and messy to assign blame and victims fear they will discover they are at fault and be humiliated.

Investors often would rather go to the crook they have a relationship with for a reassuring explanation of where their money went than entertain the notion they've been ripped off and seek out a second opinion that might sever the bond. The

SEC admits as much on its website when discussing affinity fraud: *Victims often fail to notify authorities or pursue their legal remedies and instead try to work things out within the group. Where the fraudsters have used respected community or religious leaders to convince others to join the investment, victims are inclined to accept reassurances from those leaders.*

In all things human, relationships often trump the facts. For scammers, the message is clear: Building and maintaining relationships with victims is the key to your success and defense.

> In all things human, relationships often trump the facts. For scammers, the message is clear: Building and maintaining relationships with victims is the key to your success and defense.

I've seen strong personal relationships at the center of financial dealings withstand even outrageously bad—devastating—investment losses. It makes little sense, but many investors would rather believe impersonal, unforeseeable market forces they can't understand or control caused their losses, as opposed to someone standing immediately before them who they know and could easily hold accountable.

How crazy can it get? After I had investigated and reported to a client that his family lawyer had been stealing money, the client told me that since the lawyer (when confronted with the wrongdoing) had agreed to provide free legal services in the future, i.e., "work off the debt," he wasn't going to prosecute.

"Let me get this straight," I said. "You're gonna trust a known thief to handle your legal matters—little stuff like your will or the purchase of your home—because he's going to do the work *for free* to repay the "debt" which is in fact a theft? Are you out of your mind! What's the value of legal services provided by a lawyer who has admitted to felonious activity? Something less than zero in my book. That makes as much sense as hiring a doctor who's lost his license to perform open-heart surgery because he's offering a discount!"

"But, I've known this guy for years. We're really close. I went to his son's bar mitzvah," said the client.

"In case you've forgotten, we've discovered he's been ripping you off for years. He is not your friend," I said.

Victims struggle to maintain personal relationships with perpetrators. Go figure. I've also found that people continue to respect financial firms well after those firms have lost their credibility. A Jesuit priest I sat next to on a long Greyhound bus ride to Boston when I was in law school once memorably told me, "There are some people who have educations, credentials, and reputations well beyond their capabilities."

Truth be known, all longstanding Wall Street firms have reputations far beyond their capabilities. Each of these firms—household names—has a voluminous history of wrongdoing disclosed to the public on the industry's FINRA BrokerCheck system and in SEC filings that would make a convicted serial killer blush. Trust none of them.

WEALTHY "FAMILY OFFICES"

A decade ago, I was invited to give a speech at a family office conference where professionals who are hired to manage billionaires' family money came together to discuss their employers' investments and peccadilloes. Never heard of "family offices"? Here's the low-down:

People who have amassed so much money (whether through inheritance, hard work, or both) that they are effectively in "the business" of managing their money, staff offices to manage the family wealth and tend to their unique personal needs. These uber-wealthy families often know a lot about their respective operating businesses—the businesses that made them wealthy. But when it comes to the business of managing wealth, the families know squat. Worse still, they hire as advisors veterans from the wealth management industry who are all-too-comfortable with and accepting of, corrupt standard industry practices. These former industry insiders recommend firms, such as their past employers, that end up pillaging the family fortune.

At the conference, I was trying to awaken the complacent crowd to the fact that Wall Street was not their friend. They were polite but clearly not on board with my seemingly subversive message. A voice from the audience stated, "Well, at least if I hire Goldman Sachs to manage the family money, no one can ever criticize me. They're the gold standard, right?"

Oh my. Did I really just hear what I thought I heard?

To put the statement in context, I was giving the speech shortly after Matt Taibbi of *Rolling Stone* magazine penned a lengthy and widely-discussed article, post 2008 market meltdown and Wall Street bailout, about Goldman Sachs. In the article, he referred to the firm as "a great vampire squid wrapped around the face of humanity, relentlessly jamming its blood funnel into anything that smells like money." The entire world had suddenly come to the conclusion that Goldman was evil incarnate and the firm was reeling from the bad publicity.

Goldman most trustworthy in the world to handle family wealth? You'd have to live in a galaxy light- years away for the news of Goldman's reputational nose-dive to not have reached you. Or, could it be the family office crowd lived in an alternative universe populated with rarefied beings—a world where the richest are treated especially well by Wall Street?

SOVEREIGN WEALTH FUNDS

In recent years I've been watching another class of supposedly savvy investors—sovereign wealth funds (SWFs)—make colossal blunders managing their investments.

A SWF is a state-owned investment fund that invests in real and financial assets such as stocks, bonds, real estate, precious metals, or in alternative investments such as private equity fund or hedge funds. Sovereign wealth funds invest globally.

These emerging heavyweight investors—new to Wall Street—seem to be making all the wrong moves, such as blindly trusting the same old investment powerhouses that have proven to most Americans they can't be trusted.

Worse still, SWFs (like American state and local government pensions) often get seduced into "exclusive" strategic partnerships with Wall Street's "finest." SWFs are largely unaware of concerns that are paramount to institutional investors in America today such as conflicts of interest, fiduciary duties, corruptive industry practices, undisclosed and excessive compensation arrangements, fraud, and misrepresentation and their impact upon net performance.

Scrutiny of the integrity of investment service providers to SWFs is lackluster, at best. A few years ago Libya's sovereign-investment fund filed suit against Goldman alleging devastating losses of 98% of a $1.3 billion bet on currency movements and other complex trades done with Goldman in 2008. The Libyan Investment Authority claimed that Goldman took advantage of the LIA's financial naivety by first gaining its trust, then encouraging it to make risky and ultimately worthless investments in equity derivatives. A Goldman Sachs executive footed the bill for prostitutes and the bank paid for a lavish trip to Dubai for the brother of a decision-maker at the sovereign wealth fund, a lawyer for the fund alleged.

The LIA claimed that they completely trusted Goldman and believed that its former head of North Africa was "their very close friend."

One lesson here is that when the client loses 98% of its money to you overnight, you're probably going to get sued. NEVER propose a deal that amounts to an *overnight* wealth transfer.

Recently Goldman agreed to pay a $3.9 billion settlement related to a scandal involving 1MDB, a Malaysian state investment fund that was at the center of global investigations into corruption and money laundering.

For those who aren't billionaires or sovereignties, rest assured these investors have no special market insights or edge. They get fleeced all the time by Wall Street. They're just better at hiding the damage because new money is coming in to replace the money squandered. As long as enough water pours into a leaking bucket, it will always look full.

In conclusion, scammers who maintain strong personal relationships with their clients, are skilled in explaining away bad investment performance results (more on this later), and don't conspicuously steal all the clients' money at once—only slowly bleed them over time—chances are, won't get sued.

Only a small percentage of frauds are ever detected by clients. And only a fraction of detected frauds are prosecuted.

As indicated in the Forbes article in the supplementary reading material, *Mourning Vincent "Buddy" Cianci, Rhode Island's Least Dangerous Politician*, the ex-mayor of Providence, Rhode Island, is an excellent example of a convicted felon who was nevertheless cherished by many in his community until the day of his death. As I state in the article: Believe it or not, "people skills" do matter even today—far more than debating finesse, or an impressive resume.

Scammers who:

- Maintain strong personal relationships with their clients;
- Are skilled in explaining away bad performance; and
- Don't conspicuously steal all the clients' money at once—only slowly bleed them over time—chances are, won't get sued.

Only a small percentage of frauds are ever detected by clients. And only a fraction of detected frauds are prosecuted.

17

SELL WHAT PEOPLE WANT TO BUY AND PROSPER FOREVER

The surest, fastest road to riches is to sell investors what they want to buy. I call this "the happy sale." That's a whole lot easier than selling an investment product that may be better for the consumer but isn't what they secretly desire in their heart of hearts.

As I mentioned earlier, over the course of my career I've sold forensic reviews to investors which are comparable to colonoscopies—a pain in the butt nobody wants. Forensic investigations focus upon the causes of losses, who is at fault, and assign blame. Let's call these "unhappy sales." But I've also helped create and sell financial products, e.g. mutual funds, to investors that cheerfully promise to deliver whatever rate of return the investor wants, depending on the investment strategy and risk he chooses.

Beginning in the 1980s, when I was legal counsel to one of the nation's largest mutual fund managers, the mutual fund industry was just beginning to enjoy explosive growth thanks to new Individual Retirement Account (IRA) and 401(k) legislation which more or less forced Americans to invest in costly mutual funds. After forty unremarkable years (1940-1980), the sleepy business of peddling mutual funds door-to-door was about to be jolted into hyper-drive by an intravenous mega-dose of Red Bull. In approving IRAs and 401ks, Washington lawmakers handed Wall Street on a silver platter—for the first time ever—the hard-earned retirement savings of *individual* America workers to feast upon.

Ten years later, by 1990, most employed Americans had been hoodwinked into believing that investing in over-priced, poor performing mutual funds would ensure their retirement security. The fund marketing materials, which I had a hand in drafting for my employer, were as moronic as a "Dial Your Own Return" wheel of fortune that showed the names of mutual funds in which to invest to receive the rate of return of your dreams. Twelve percent per year was doable if you invested in the right funds, investors were assured. (My job at the SEC and later at the mutual fund company was to make sure that it was disclosed—albeit in fine print—that a portion of the so-called "return" was, in fact, a return of principal, i.e., the investor's own money being returned to him disguised as investment income.)

Financial planning is as simple as that, America. Just "pick your paycheck," said the marketers at the nation's mutual fund families.

If a museum of financial advertising existed—and I think it should—it would bear witness to decades of preposterous lying by Wall Street financial terrorists.

Online Museum of Financial Advertising?

Creating an online museum of financial services advertising would be easy since the Advertising Regulation Department of FINRA, the securities industry self-regulator, reviews securities firms' advertisements and other communications with the public supposedly "to ensure that they are fair, balanced, and not misleading. Every year, the department reviews more than 100,000 communications. Firms submit communications for review either as required by FINRA's rules or on a voluntary basis. In addition, the department conducts targeted examinations and reviews communications submitted as a complaint or inquiry from a third party such as a competitor or another regulator, including FINRA staff involved in an exam."

My suggestion: To combat fraud, make the advertising files and FINRA responses to proposed ads public online.

It would take almost thirty years—a generation and a half—for Baby Boomers and Generation Xers to awaken to just how badly they'd been screwed by the mutual fund industry.

The failure of 401ks was foreseen decades ago by experts—including me. In 2003, I was asked to testify before the US Senate Banking Committee when the first wave of revelations of decades of scandalous mutual fund industry behavior—skimming from customer accounts that continues through this day—finally surfaced.

By 2008, when the impact of the near-collapse of the financial markets, coupled with the mutual fund industry's decades of gorging on workers' savings was being deeply felt, I drafted a 401k Safety Recall notice (using a children's toy Recall issued by the Consumer Product Safety Commission as my template) and sent it out as a press release to draw attention to the structural flaws and systemic abuses.

401ks were so deeply defective they should be recalled, I said.

I also published an extensive research paper, *Secrets of the 401k industry: How Employers and Mutual fund Advisers Prospered as Workers' Dreams of Retirement Security Evaporated,*[18] which documented the corrupt industry practices that played a significant role in creating the retirement crisis the nation faces today. My research revealed that while 80% of employers believed 401ks were effective in recruiting employees to come work for them, only 13% of employers believed that the 401k plans they offered would provide retirement security for their workers.

In other words, employers withheld the truth from, or lied to, workers about the probable outcome of a lifetime of faithful service and diligently contributing to their so-called retirement plans. Too frail to work, too poor to retire was likely to be the "new normal" for workers putting savings aside in 401ks. Workers' golden years would almost certainly be less than shimmering, employers had long secretly known. Realistic projected retirement outcomes weren't going to make anyone happy. But lying would.

Bottomline: Making the "happy sale," promising investors their financial goals—their retirement dreams—are reachable, is much, much, easier, more fun, and much, much, more profitable.

As in all sales, you need to understand the buyer's goals and structure your product, as well as tailor your sales pitch accordingly.

Marketing an investment product is not like selling a tangible—a car, house, or dishwasher—where the value or utility of the item is fairly apparent. The workings of these commonplace tangibles are well understood and the future satisfaction they will deliver to buyers is readily apparent.

Very few buyers of intangible investment products understand what they're buying. They may think and say they do. Regulators

---

[18]   https://www.benchmarkalert.com/wp-content/uploads/2020/07/Secrets-of-the-401k-Industry.pdf

and judges may say or believe that as long as the disclosures are adequate, investors are knowledgeable or even "sophisticated." But the truth is only a very small minority of, say, mutual fund investors, have a clue about how these investments are structured, regulated, and managed. Investments are complex and disclosures are so overwhelming that investors almost never read them.

Not surprising, given this lack of sophistication few investors have reasonable expectations regarding how the products in which they invest will perform.

So, what do investors want? What do you need to offer to make them happy?

Obviously, all investors want to make money. The question is how much and how quickly? Despite whatever the investor may say, is he looking for a reasonable rate of return over time or does he dream of becoming rich overnight? Most alluring and easiest to sell is the dream of outrageous riches.

You will need to come up with an investment theory or fiction which appeals to the dreams of your victims and makes you money regardless of the outcome. If the investor loses money (but hopefully, not all his money overnight), that's really not your problem—you walk away wealthier. Heads or tails, the savvy scammer never loses. So, think seriously about what the investor *wants* to hear.

Bear in mind that people will give you their money even when they know or suspect you may be lying to them—as long as it's a lie they want to be told.

For example, decades ago when I was in my early thirties, single and living in Manhattan, a bum on a subway platform early one morning approached me on my way to work.

"You look *great*," he cheerfully said.

He then held out a weathered paper cup, and said, "You don't have to be a Rockefella to help a fella" and grinned widely.

I laughed and gave him a dollar—fully aware that he had played me. He'd made me feel better about my appearance early one tired morning (when I really needed uplifting) and made me laugh.

Very few buyers of intangible investment products understand what they're buying. They may think and say they do. Regulators and judges may say or believe that as long as the disclosures are adequate, investors are knowledgeable or even "sophisticated." But, the truth is only a very small minority of investors have a clue about how investments are structured, regulated, and managed. Investments are complex and disclosures are so overwhelming that investors almost never read them.

Private banks and other financial institutions that cater to the wealthy play the same game. These firms stroke client egos providing "red carpet" treatment which assures clients they are successful, special, and deserving of the best life has to offer—even as they fleece them.

Deep down, the clients suspect they're being had but all the ass-kissing and lies feel sooooo good.

As I wrote in *Forbes* nearly a decade ago:

Private banks make sense if you're willing to pay through the nose for the plush carpeting and fine china—but don't kid yourself into thinking private banks will provide you with world-class fiduciary guidance or superior investment results. Most won't.

The notorious Madoff case revealed two other dimensions of feel-good marketing working in tandem: exclusivity and entitlement. Madoff so successfully used exclusivity as bait that investors, including supposedly sophisticated wealth management intermediaries, were begging to gain access to his Ponzi scheme.

"Exclusivity pitches" play upon emotions—ego and greed—which cause investors to drop their guards. If you can make the investor feel special, like the "average" doesn't apply to him because he is a member of an exclusive group, then you can easily convince him he is entitled to a special higher rate of return that otherwise might seem unrealistic.

That is, special rates for especially entitled investors.

Madoff's steady, reliable, never-miss, double-digit returns might have been "red flags" his performance was fake. But thanks to the exclusivity pitch, investors were willing to believe he could consistently deliver positive returns for the select few using a complex "split-strike conversion strategy" which no client fully understood.

While all investors want to make money and dream of becoming rich, Madoff realized his prospects would be suspicious of outrageously high returns related to mundane investment strategies. So, his fictitious investment returns were not so high as to be unbelievable and his bogus investment strategy was incomprehensibly complex. In structuring your scam, determine whether your investors are dumb enough to believe in outrageous get-rich-quick schemes (e.g. gold mines) or are more cautious and require a sophisticated scam involving moderate returns and arcane, secretive investment strategies like Madoff's. Whether you offer an outlandish get-rich-quick scheme or a complex get-rich-slowly-over-time scheme, adding in the "exclusivity pitch" will only make it more appealing.

When I served as an expert witness in Madoff litigations here's what I had to say in my testimony about the multiple "red flags" that were overlooked by Madoff investors who had for decades been satisfied customers:

"First, the investment returns related to Madoff's investment strategy were too good to be true. Managers that followed the same 'split-strike conversion' strategy did not achieve comparable results. Professionals that specifically tried to replicate Madoff's results using the same strategy could not. As Harry Markopolis, a derivatives analyst in Boston who reviewed Madoff's investment strategy in a November 2005 letter to the SEC noted, the normal return from using the 'split-strike conversion' strategy would approximate the return on Treasury Bills—far less than Madoff's claimed returns. Moreover, Madoff's claim to a positive return in virtually every month over a fifteen-year plus period is so unlikely as to be evidence of fraud in and of itself.

Second, critical to Madoff's purported investment strategy was the purchase and sale of put and call options on the billions of dollars of securities under management. Given the enormous amount of the assets under management at Madoff purportedly invested in the strategy and the level of options trading required to implement the strategy, there were not enough listed and over-the-counter index options to support Madoff's level of trading. Further, the large volume of option trades that the strategy would have generated would have had a profound impact upon the market. Likewise, there is no evidence of the substantial block trades of the securities in Madoff's purported strategy that would have been required. Further, press accounts indicate that even a cursory analysis of the stock trades reported on an account statement compared against the actual trading prices on the relevant date would have shown that the prices did not match."

Granted, the above two "red flags" require a level of investment sophistication few investors possess, as well as some research capability. On the other hand, most of the following "red flags" require nothing more than common sense—another quality which investors generally lack.

"Third, Madoff's requirement that his customers custody their assets at his firm, as opposed to at a third-party custodian was unusual and posed real dangers, including lack of independent verification of assets within accounts and related returns.

Fourth, Madoff's auditor was a three-person firm, which would not have had the expertise to audit an adviser with $50 billion in reported assets.

Fifth, the form of the Madoff statements was outdated and lacking in detail.

Sixth, other investment managers noted inconsistencies between customer account statements and the audited financial statements Madoff filed with the SEC. The stock holdings reported in the Madoff quarterly statements with the SEC appeared too small to support the size of the assets Madoff claimed to be managing.

Seventh, the degree of secrecy insisted upon by Madoff was highly unusual and suspicious. While successful investment managers generally seek to tout their level of assets under management and their investment strategy and to be responsive to increasing demands for transparency, Madoff's refusal to provide information raised serious concerns with some cautious managers and advisors.

Equally important, the fee arrangement between Madoff and the 'feeder firms' was the opposite of convention and counter-intuitive: the investment fund manager who generated the exceptional returns was paid a low commission-based fee and the marketing firms received rich performance-like fees. All of these enormous fees were paid to the 'feeder firms' for what was essentially marketing Madoff. Madoff's willingness to part with such rich fees, which ordinarily would be retained by the investment manager, not the marketer, is a blatant 'red flag.'

Finally, there were financial industry publications that raised concerns. These published reports are significant because, in my experience, while the financial press may comment on investment manager strategy or performance, there is an understandable reluctance to question the integrity of a manager. Consequently, when articles of such a nature do appear, it is exceptional and requires immediate attention on the part of fiduciaries responsible for safeguarding client assets.

It should be noted that the media who reported the suspicions of Madoff's possible criminal activity were not in a position to gain access to Madoff's trading records to confirm their suspicions. Madoff's clients, on the other hand, could have but didn't."

In conclusion, you don't want to run a Ponzi scheme like Madoff and risk being sentenced to 150 years in prison. You don't have to, to be a fabulously successful scammer. Had Madoff actually invested at least some of the money he was given by clients—regardless of whether or not he lost it—he would still be wealthy, free to spend the money he'd stole. He could have stayed in Vail, not gone to jail. Madoff is not your mentor.

But you can learn a lot from fraudsters like Madoff, particularly about marketing investment products. Madoff and other big-time scammers may know little or nothing about investing but clearly are skilled at getting investors to believe the improbable, trust them, and fork over their money.

18

CHARGE HIGH FEES, PAY FOR MARKETING MUSCLE, SELL MORE THAN EVER!

Conventional wisdom has it that "you get what you pay for." In other words, the more you pay, the more you get for your money. Nothing could be further from the truth when it comes to investing. Since advisors that charge high fees have a difficult time adding enough value to overcome the additional expense, investors who pay more...actually get less.

> Conventional wisdom has it that "you get what you pay for." Nothing could be further from the truth when it comes to investing.

Unlike most other industries, the fees investment funds and advisers charge investors for *comparable* services *vary astronomically*.

Passive, or index investment management services, can be purchased by institutional investors for 1 basis point (one one-hundredth of a percent) or even "for free."[19] Active managers, who attempt to beat the market by stock-picking, often charge fees that are 100 times greater (1 percent). Alternative

---

[19]   Certain index managers will manage large accounts at no cost, in exchange for securities lending income related to the portfolio.

investment managers, including hedge, venture, and private equity, may charge asset-based, performance, and other fees amounting to approximately 7 percent—700 times greater than indexing. Alternative investments structured as "fund of funds" or "manager of managers" involve additional layers of fees (2 percent) paid to underlying investment managers, for a grand total of nearly 10 percent.

Paying higher fees for active traditional stock-picking or investing in alternative assets does not guarantee and, in fact, *negatively correlates* to superior investment performance. Indeed, the overwhelming majority of active managers fail to outperform market indexes over time net of fees. The higher the fees, the greater the drag on investment returns and less that's left for the investor.

Paying high fees is like running a race with sandbags tied to your ankles: you might win but you're going to have to work a whole lot harder.

In short, less expensive investments generally outperform those richly priced—just as low-cost digital and electric watches tell better time than Rolexes costing tens of thousands of dollars more.

As a jeweler once told me, "If you want a watch that tells great time, buy a Seiko. If you want a beautiful piece of jewelry, buy a Rolex."

But most investors pay little attention to fees. "Why should I care about the fees, as long as I'm making money?" is a typical investor attitude. Savvy investors, on the other hand, know that it's impossible to predict how well an investment will perform in the future. They know the only variable they can control is the fees they pay.

Every investment has a cost and there are many different kinds of costs or expenses, including asset-based fees, brokerage commissions, and custody and organizational expenses. They all have one thing in common: If the money is going somewhere else, it's not going to you, warns mutual fund giant Vanguard.

So, costs matter a lot, says Vanguard.

"They might not seem significant, but they add up, compounding along with your investment returns. In other words, you don't just lose the tiny amount of fees you pay—you also lose all the growth that money might have had for years into the future.

Imagine you have $100,000 invested. If the account earned 6% a year for the next 25 years and had no costs or fees, you'd end up with about $430,000.

If, on the other hand, you paid 2% a year in costs, after 25 years you'd only have about $260,000.

That's right: The 2% you paid every year would wipe out almost 40% of your final account value. 2% doesn't sound so small anymore, does it?"

As a result of this indifference about expenses and focus upon promised investment returns, investors are generally unaware of the totality of fees they pay.

Even the largest, supposedly most sophisticated pensions are clueless about fees. Not only do they not care enough to closely monitor their total fees, they routinely lie about, i.e., understate, how much they pay Wall Street to manage their assets. They typically pay exponentially more—perhaps ten times more—than they report to the public.

In countless investigations, I have proven the fees pensions disclose to the public are just the "tip of the iceberg."

For example, from the beaches of sunny South Florida a quick peek at the website of the distant —nearly 1,500 miles away—$7 billion Employee Retirement System of the State of Rhode Island[20] led me to conclude in 2013 that the investment fees the pension was paying to Wall Street were suddenly skyrocketing. Worse still, the state pension was hiding its escalating fees from the public. Rhode Island politicians and pension officials were dramatically understating the total expenses.

At that time, April 2013, the total investment management fees disclosed on the state pension's website was **$11,563,979**.

Remember that number.

---

[20]   http://investments.treasury.ri.gov/

A hastily penned article in *Forbes* entitled "Rhode Island Public Pension 'Reform' Looks More Like Wall Street Feeding Frenzy"[21] stating my alarming findings drew an immediate and harsh response from the clueless politician responsible for the pension at that time, Rhode Island General Treasurer Gina Raimondo.

The following day, Raimondo admitted in an interview/article entitled, "Raimondo Fires Back After *Forbes* Contributor Attacks Her,"[22] that she did not know the amount of the fees the pension paid to its investment managers. Nevertheless, despite her lack of knowledge, she assured readers that the total disclosed and still-undisclosed fees were reasonable.

The article could have been more aptly titled *Raimondo Misfires* because the state Treasurer had a legal duty to make sure the fees the state pension paid Wall Street money managers for investment services were reasonable. If Raimondo and the pension officials *did not even know* the amount of fees the pension paid, they could not possibly have concluded the fees were reasonable, consistent with their legal obligations.

Not surprising, the disclosure regarding investment expenses on the pension's website was swiftly modified in response to my observations and growing criticism. By August, **$47.5 million** in total fees was disclosed—a 400% exponential increase.[23] By September, the disclosed fees mushroomed to **$70 million.**[24] Today total annual fees disclosed by the pension are nearly **$80 million.**

---

21 https://www.forbes.com/sites/edwardsiedle/2013/04/04/rhode-island-public-pension-reform-looks-more-like-wall-street-feeding-frenzy/#61d5bdde879d

22 https://www.wpri.com/blog/2013/04/05/qa-raimondo-fires-back-after-attack-by-forbes-contributor/

23 https://www.providencejournal.com/article/20130803/NEWS/308039987

24 https://www.providencejournal.com/article/20130925/News/309259970

To recap, amid growing scrutiny by independent experts, the fees disclosed to the public ballooned—in less than a year—from **$11.5 million to $80 million annually.**

These totals are *closer* to the truth.

But as I concluded six years ago in the findings of my October 2013 forensic investigation, *Rhode Island Public Pension Reform: Wall Street's License to Steal,*[25] "the total investment expenses may already, or in the near future, amount to a staggering almost **$100 million** annually." Worse still, the pension did not get what it paid for—investment performance plummeted as fees soared.

The $87 billion North Carolina state pension is ten times bigger than tiny Rhode Island's. Surely the eleventh largest public pension fund in the United States providing retirement benefits for more than 875,000 North Carolinians, including teachers, state employees, firefighters, police officers, and other public workers has the resources to properly calculate and disclose the investment fees it pays—assuming, of course, it cared and wanted to tell the public the truth.

My 2014 forensic investigation of the state pension entitled *North Carolina Pension's Secretive Alternative Investment Gamble: A Sole Fiduciary's Failed 'Experiment,'* concluded the state Treasurer had withheld from public disclosure a massive portion of the fees the pension paid its highest-risk money managers, resulting in the dramatic understatement of fees and risks related to certain investments, as well as the pension as a whole. Indeed, it appeared that the massive hidden fees she failed to disclose in many instances dwarfed the excessive fees disclosed to the public.

The limited investment fee information provided to me by the Treasurer indicated that disclosed fees had ballooned over 1,000 percent since 2000, as the pension moved away from low-cost, low-risk internally managed investments to high-cost, high-risk alternative funds managed by Wall Street. The total disclosed

---

[25] https://www.forbes.com/sites/edwardsiedle/2013/10/18/rhode-island-public-pension-reform-wall-streets-license-to-steal/#4e94799e7659

investment fees were projected to climb to over **$500 million**. I estimated the total *undisclosed* fees would comparably climb to approximately **$500 million**.

Thus, I estimated total state pension annual fees would amount to approximately **$1 billion** in the near future—almost twice the figure projected and disclosed by the then-Treasurer.

The fact that most investors couldn't care less about fees and expenses is, of course, fantastic news for investment scammers!

> As a general rule, higher fee products pay greater marketing incentives to sales intermediaries and greater marketing muscle results in greater sales.
>
> Do not hesitate to pay others handsomely to recommend, as well as defend your product out of the tens of thousands offered in the marketplace.

As a scammer, you want to charge the highest fees you can for your services both because that's more money in your pocket and also because that's more money you have to share with, or pay to, others to market your crappy product (which means even more money in your pocket). As you grow your fraud, you want to incentivize others to steer investors into your fund. Don't be stingy. Get them excited to be working for you. Not only will these intermediaries help sell your product, they are your initial line of defense should investors become unhappy and start grumbling. More often than not, they'll be able to talk angry investors out of suing you. So, pay others handsomely to recommend, as well as defend your product out of the tens of thousands offered in the marketplace.

As a general rule, higher fee products offer greater marketing incentives and greater marketing muscle results in greater sales. If more advertising didn't result in greater sales, then no one would advertise, right?

Every Wall Streeter wants to sell variable annuities, hedge, and private equity funds because these high-cost products offer lavish fee-sharing and commissions. Likewise, advisers and brokers rarely recommend better-performing index funds which pay miniscule commissions. They dread clients who specifically ask for passively managed investments. In my experience, low-cost index funds are only found in client portfolios if the client has specifically asked for them or if they are coupled with high-cost products that more than make up for the revenue loss to the adviser related to indexing.

Once again, the Madoff case offers insights into investment product marketing. The greatest fees were paid to the "feeder firms" for little more than marketing Madoff.

In conclusion, remember that investors rarely care about the fees they pay—only the riches they hope to earn. So, feel free to charge super high fees—you'll need the extra money. As you grow your scam you're going to need the help of others to recommend it and steer clients your way. Be generous with them and they will sing your praises, as well as defend you when questions arise.

Wall Street history is replete with examples of great products which didn't sell well, and terrible schemes that sold like hotcakes—despite their dismal results. Building rich fees into your investment product to be shared with others who assist in the marketing is the best way of ensuring you're a winner, not a loser.

19

HOW TO MAKE YOUR INVESTMENT PERFORMANCE LOOK GREAT

Investors scurry to advisers who, they believe, will deliver superior investment performance, i.e., make them richer.

Therefore, to succeed as an investment professional, you've either got to be that one-in-a-million investment genius who regularly delivers outstanding performance, or you have to figure out how to *appear* to be that genius—without outright lying like Bernie Madoff and being sentenced to 150 years in federal prison.

Bear in mind, even the world's best investors eventually underperform—have losing streaks—before hopefully returning to beat the market. For example, legendary investor Warren Buffett, who has beaten the S&P 500 for decades, has massively underperformed over the past year and lagged the market since the beginning of 2009. Yet, for the past eleven years, investors have kept the faith in, and their money invested with, him.

So, investment savant or not, if you're going to prosper in this business, you need to be able to convince investors you're a winner to get them to initially invest and then stay with you during the lean years when your performance isn't winning. Here's what the CFA Institute, a global association for investment professionals had to say about the importance of persuasive performance explanations:

"Whether markets are rising or falling, resilient investment organizations value highly qualified performance professionals.

Indeed, there is a curious countercyclicality to the demand for their expertise: **It is when results are most disappointing that cogent explanations are most urgently needed** (emphasis added)."[26]

Chances are, you are not one of the world's best investors and never will be. But, as I've said ad nauseam, you don't have to be a top stock-picker to profit handsomely in this racket.

The very fact that the overwhelming majority of people employed on Wall Street and at most of the largest, highly profitable firms are not savvy investors should be very encouraging to you.

I learned that remarkable truth decades ago when I, at a very young age, was legal counsel to one of the largest money managers in the world.

DON'T JUST DO SOMETHING, SIT THERE

Back then—in the 1980s—money was rolling into mutual funds so quickly that I and a handful of senior managers were hastily hired by my employer in Boston to handle the burgeoning business. We were temporarily housed at the pricey Four Seasons Hotel overlooking Boston's historic public garden.

Since I was young, single, and new to the corporate world, my first year I partied with my co-workers in the evenings after work, and on weekends cross-country skied outside the city, rock climbed in New Hampshire, and soaked in the hotel's penthouse hot tub—pushing to extreme limits the company's generous relocation package. Times were good for my employer, and I was having a good time...on my employer.

Socializing with the mutual fund portfolio managers, each of whom managed billions in their respective funds, as well as marketers who pushed the firm's investment products out to retail brokerages selling to the public, gave me invaluable insight as to

---

[26]   Investment Performance Measurement: Evaluating and Presenting Results, Phillip Lawton, Todd Jankowski.

how the game was played—knowledge about the real world of managing money which supplemented what I learned in my role as the company's lawyer and compliance director.

If you're the in-house lawyer to a Wall Street firm, the unspoken rule is that you're supposed to stay in your office with the door, your mouth, and your eyes shut. That's your job.

Don't just do something, sit there.

Unless, of course, someone with authority comes knocking on your closed office door with a matter for you to address. Even then, you want to be careful you don't go prying into things your employer doesn't want you to discover. Best to check with those members of senior management who hired (and have the power to fire) you before responding to any request from the rank and file.

Hear no evil, see no evil, speak no evil. That's the glide-path to a long and relatively profitable in-house corporate legal career.

Fraternizing with co-workers—worse still, pounding drinks with them after work at the elegant bar at Le Meridien Hotel in the classically designed former Federal Reserve Bank of Boston building steps from and connected to the firm's offices—was, I would soon learn, high-risk corporate behavior.

What I learned boozing with freely-speaking portfolio managers after-hours was that the so-called "investment process" at many of the largest mutual fund companies really amounts to nothing more than what is commonly referred to in the industry as "closet indexing."

I won't go into the details but basically an investment firm comes up with a list of "approved" stocks derived from, say, those included in the S&P 500 Index. From this universe of stocks approved for the managers to buy on behalf of client portfolios, the domestic equity managers are permitted to select those which they want for the portfolios they manage and exclude others. This approach to managing money is called a "team" versus the "star" system of managing money.

The team system not only ensures that the investment performances of all the mutual funds within a fund complex more-or-less track the benchmark indices the funds will be judged against, but also that no single portfolio manager outperforms the others, emerges as a super-star, and might be tempted to jump-ship, taking his client assets with him.

Sure, a "team" approach likely results in mediocre investment performance for your clients, but it ensures predictable revenues for your money management company—which is, of course, why you're in the business, right?

The point is that even a moron can manage a closet index fund. It's as simple as baking a cake—buying and selling stocks more or less in the same amounts as the index recipe stipulates. Closet indexing is viewed negatively by investors because they are paying a so-called "professional" a 1% fee to actively pick stocks for them when they could simply choose a passively-managed index fund and pay a 1 basis point fee or 99% less. Also, it's called "closet" indexing because the managers who use this ruse do not publicly disclose the practice. They claim to be stock-pickers.

There are plenty of other simple investment strategies that will ensure that you—as a scammer—don't horrifically underperform the market and lose all your clients' money through investment missteps or client defections.

The least of your concerns should be who will manage the money you persuade investors to hand over to you. You can even hire an established money management firm as a sub-adviser, or subcontractor, to manage the money you raise. Anything's possible when you can talk people into letting you manage their money.

The key is, once you've got ahold of people's money don't get greedy. If you can resist the temptation to steal too much, too soon, you're on easy street for years to come.

To be a professional financial adviser, you have to get ahold of other people's money.

A money manager without money to manage is not a money manager. In other words, you've got to get ahold of Other People's Money (OPM) to get in the game. Once you do, you're in. It's that simple. Once you've got their money, the goal is to hang onto it as long as possible to effectuate the "wealth transfer."

No need for impressive credentials.

You don't need an MBA from Harvard, a PhD in Economics from Princeton, or any other professional credential to manage OPM. In fact, some of the most highly credentialed people that ever got into the asset management business have crashed and burned.

Ever heard of Long Term Capital Management, the hedge fund that had two Nobel laureates on its board whose spectacular collapse required financial intervention by the Federal Reserve to prevent catastrophic losses throughout the financial system? So much for "smarts."

Only selling skills required.

On the other hand, some of the worst investment advisers have made a fortune—for themselves, off their clients.

The truth be known, many of the world's leading asset management firms, household names with trillions of assets under management, are poor-to-mediocre investors. What they're very good at is *marketing*.

As in many fields of endeavor, salesmanship is the key determinant of success in money management.

MANIPULATING YOUR PERFORMANCE RESULTS

While you don't have to be any good at investing, to be effective in marketing your investment product or services, you need to be skilled at discussing and presenting your investment performance results in the most favorable light.

So, you've got to learn how to massage or manipulate your investment performance results aka "track record" to:

1. Lure them in: Advertise or present performance that leads prospective clients to believe you have in the past and will in the future deliver superior investment results; and

2. Keep them in no matter what: Learn to present your performance to existing clients, including explaining away your less-than-stellar results. Again, there's really no getting around the need to be able to defend bad results, given the nature of the asset management business. That is, stock market efficiency theoretically makes consistent outperformance impossible. Sooner or later, you're going to be in a slump.

Learning to manipulate your investment performance results is easy because regulators and industry groups have over the decades developed extensive standards (volumes) for *fairly* presenting investment performance which, of course, the industry regularly skirts when the need arises.

Anyone who understands how to *fairly* present or disclose performance to investors must know how to *unfairly* manipulate investment results, right?

It's as simple as doing what you're not supposed to do but with appropriate disclosures the investor will neither read nor understand. For example:

1. Include only winning client accounts in your performance results (i.e., "cherry-pick" accounts).

Similarly, many mutual fund managers will "seed" or incubate multiple new fund accounts and offer to the public only the fund account that performs well. The losers never see the light of day. Here's how it's done: Open three accounts with $10,000 in each. Invest the $10,000 in each account in a different asset class, e.g., domestic stocks, domestic bonds, and foreign stocks. At the end of the year, see which of the three seeded funds has done well and which have done badly. Tell the world about the good fund(s) and shutter the bad. You now have an investment fund with a legitimate track record that you can market to investors. You have demonstrated that you know how to manage money.

2. Compare your performance to some easily beatable, inappropriate benchmark (i.e., an apples-to-oranges comparison). For example, compare a risky stock fund to a risk-free T-bill rate of return. Or don't compare your performance to anything—just joyfully announce, "We're up 10%!" Don't mention the stock market was up 15% for the year. (In a sharply rising market, clients will be satisfied they had a solid positive return and overlook the fact you underperformed the market. On the other hand, if the market's down 20%, you'll have difficulty convincing clients a 10% loss is good and may have to spin your performance results another way.)

3. Show your performance only over the most favorable time periods (i.e., cherry-pick time periods). For example, if your 3-, 5-, and 10-year results stink but your 1-year performance is acceptable, prominently advertise the 1-year results. Accentuate the positive, ignore or bury the negative.

4. Invest client monies in so-called "hard-to-value" alternative assets, the values and performance of which you may—legally—inflate. (More on this in the next chapter.)

My personal favorite is using hypothetical back-tested (HBP) performance over a hypothetical period of time, developed with the benefit of hindsight and without any actual money at risk. In other words, use a performance record developed by applying a particular investment strategy to historic financial data. The back-tested results show investment decisions that theoretically would have been made had the given strategy been employed during the particular past period of time. The use of HBP is highly misleading but since there is no rule specifically prohibiting its use, it is common in the industry and won't land you in the hoosegow.

For example, decades ago I listened to a sales pitch for a new mutual fund that would invest only in companies based in St. Louis, Missouri. Supposedly, over the previous decade, publicly-traded companies headquartered in the city outperformed the national average. Whether St. Louis-based corporations would continue to outperform the market over the next ten years was unknown (and seemed unlikely to me) but there were probably plenty of investors—particularly in St. Louis, I suspect—willing to wager they would.

IT'S ALL IN THE FINE PRINT

With respect to all of the above machinations, the more disclosure you provide, the less likely you'll be prosecuted. Likewise, the lengthier the disclosure, the less likely anyone will bother to read it. Keep your disclosure unintelligible gibberish, hard-to-find (e.g. in a footnote at the end of the document), and in teensy weensy micro-print.

For example, hypothetical investment results advertised to the public are the trickiest of all and require disclosure footnotes such as:

- The results do not represent the results of actual trading using client assets but were achieved by means of the retroactive application of a model that was designed with the benefit of hindsight.

- The returns should not be considered indicative of the skill of the adviser.
- The results may not reflect the impact that any material market or economic factors might have had on the adviser's use of the back-tested model if the model had been used during the period to actually manage client assets.
- The adviser, during the period in question, was either not managing money at all, or none according to the strategy depicted.

Sure, all those warnings should scare any rational investor away but, don't worry, few will read them.

If you can lead the client to believe whatever performance you deliver—the pennies he gets after you've taken your hefty share—is, in fact, desirable or acceptable, then you've got a license to steal. You will never be poor.

Learning to manipulate your investment performance results is easy because regulators and industry groups have over the decades developed extensive standards for *fairly* presenting investment performance which, of course, the industry regularly skirts when the need arises.

Anyone who understands how to *fairly* present or disclose performance to investors must know how to *unfairly* manipulate investment results, right?

It's as simple as doing what you're not supposed to do but with appropriate disclosures

20

WHEN YOU VALUE THE ASSETS, YOU'RE ALWAYS ADDING VALUE

In the previous chapter I said, given the nature of the investment management business—i.e., the fact that even the best money managers underperform the market from time to time—you must learn how to defend and explain away bad performance if you're going to prosper. That's not entirely true.

There is a notable, and growing, exception to the rule that poor investment performance is inevitable.

Q: How can you be sure the investments you make on behalf of clients always go up in value and at least meet the market, if not beat it?

A: Invest only in hard-to-value private or alternative assets!

This is the only one sure—perfectly legal—way for a money manager to be certain he will *always* be able to report superior investment results to his clients. Now, let me explain how this is possible.

"TRADITIONAL" VERSUS "ALTERNATIVE" ASSETS

By way of background, money managers invest client monies in assets which rise and fall in value over time. The idea is to buy low and later sell at a higher price, realizing a profit.

"Traditional" assets, like stocks and bonds, are bought and sold in public markets—e.g., the New York Stock Exchange—where prices of assets are widely quoted and published daily, hourly, and minute-by-minute throughout the trading day.

A manager of "traditional" stock and bond assets cannot get away with claiming the values of publicly-traded stocks he bought for clients, e.g., Apple or Google, are higher than the quoted prices. Therefore, unless he presciently bought at lower than the current price, he's a loser.

So, this is not a sandbox the savvy scammer wants to play in.

Scammers need to steer clear of fully transparent, highly-liquid, publicly-traded stocks and bonds.

However, "alternative" assets that are not publicly-traded and therefore lack clear-cut, readily ascertainable values—like real estate, venture capital, and private equity, are tailor-made for scamming. Because these assets are arguably hard-to-value, they are ripe for price manipulation, i.e., inflation of their values by you.

Believe it or not, private equity and other managers of so-called "alternative assets" are generally free, under applicable law, to determine by themselves the value of these assets. They get to decide how much the "stuff" they bought for clients is worth. The more the stuff in client portfolios is worth, the better the money manager's performance is, the more clients that flock to him, the more the adviser gets paid! This is because money managers are paid on a percentage of client assets under management basis. So, when the manager *claims* the portfolio's value has doubled, his fee doubles.

Allowing these "alternative" managers to determine the value of hard-to-value assets makes no sense, of course, because the manager is subject to an outrageous conflict of interest when he does so. As a result, a few savvy sophisticated investors and regulators demand third-party, independent valuations of hard-to-value investments. But there is no such legal requirement.

A manager of traditional stock and bond assets cannot get away with claiming the values of publicly-traded stocks are higher than the quoted prices.

So, this is not a sandbox the savvy scammer wants to play in.

However, assets that are not publicly-traded and therefore lack clear-cut, readily ascertainable values—like real estate, venture capital, and private equity, are tailor-made for scamming.

Below is typical language private equity managers use to disclose this valuation scam. As you can see, the firms are not hiding anything.

"Generally, the Adviser will determine the value of all of a Fund's investments for which market quotations are available based on publicly available quotations. However, market quotations will not be available for most of a Fund's investments because, among other things, the securities of portfolio companies held by such Fund generally will be illiquid and not quoted on any exchange. The Adviser will determine the value of all the Fund's investments that are not readily marketable. However, the process of valuing securities for which reliable market quotations are not available is based on inherent uncertainties and the resulting values may differ from values that would have been determined had an active market existed for such securities and may differ from the prices at which such securities ultimately may be sold. There can be no assurance that the Adviser will have all the information necessary to make valuation decisions in respect of these investments, or that any information provided by third parties on which such decisions are based will be correct. There can be no assurance that the valuation decision of the Adviser with respect to an investment will represent the value realized by the relevant Fund on the eventual disposition of such investment or that would, in fact, be realized upon an immediate disposition of such investment on the date of its valuation. In addition, the exercise of discretion in valuation by the General Partner may give rise to conflicts of interest, including in connection with determining the amount and timing of distributions of carried interest and the calculation of management fees."

It's all disclosed: Most investments will lack market values, so we'll make up values and the values we make up may not be real. Oh, and by the way, we have a conflict of interest when we make up the values. When we lie, we get paid more.

As good as this legalized lying sounds, it gets better. You are allowed to play this game—inflating the prices of assets in client portfolios—*in secrecy*, withholding from your investors the nature of the assets you have purchased on their behalf.

Since you don't even have to tell them the crap they're invested in, they can't possibly question or verify the bullshit values you have made up!

For example, an amateurish private equity fund I was investigating in Nashville had invested my pension client's money in a small local chicken farm and a sausage factory. What's the value of a small local chicken farm, or sausage factory? God only knows. Who's going to buy it from you? When I asked the investment manager what his "exit strategy" was—i.e., how he was going to profit from the two investments, long-term—he hadn't a clue.

"What are you going to do," I jokingly said, "merge the companies and make chicken sausage?"

At Berkshire Hathaway 2019 annual meeting, Warren Buffett, the Oracle of Omaha, made a point of criticizing private equity money managers whose reported investment "returns are not really calculated in a manner that I would regard as honest."[27]

That's a really nice way of saying these guys are fucking liars.

In conclusion, scammers should invest all client money in "alternative" assets for which market quotations will not be

---

[27] https://www.bloomberg.com/news/articles/2019-05-05/ private-equity-s-returns-questioned-again-this-time-by-buffett

available because they are illiquid and not quoted on any exchange. Warn clients these investments are hard-to-value; you will unilaterally determine the value of all such investments on your own; the process of valuing securities for which reliable market quotations are not available is inherently uncertain; and that you are subject to a conflict of interest in creating these fictional values because the more they're worth, the more you get paid.

Mark up the value on every investment you purchase and keep the value higher than the market no matter what happens. This will ensure your performance always looks competitive and that the asset-based fees you get paid stay high.

Keep secret the nature of the investments you have made to ensure no one gets wise to the game you're playing. Transparency is always the scammer's enemy, secrecy his friend.

> Transparency is always the scammer's enemy, secrecy his friend.

21

LET ME HELP YOU SELL YOUR CRAPPY PRODUCT TO THE DUMBEST INVESTORS

BY CHRISTOPHER TOBE, CFA, CAIA

My name is Christopher Tobe and I am a registered investment advisor and former Trustee of the $15 billion Kentucky state pension. The Kentucky pension is, at this very moment, in the midst of a groundbreaking lawsuit alleging investment wrongdoing. When I was on the pension board, I was a whistleblower who reported my concerns about the pension to the SEC.

I am often asked by scammers peddling dubious investment schemes how to get state and local government pensions to invest in their crap. It's no secret that these pensions are generally the dumbest investors in the room, so plenty of Wall Street fraudsters want a piece of that stupid money.

Here's how these conversations would go—if the scammers were telling the unvarnished truth.

Mr. Wall Street: I have created a high-cost, high-risk private equity investment fund and I want to get fabulously rich. I want to tell investors that the fees I charge are around 3% but I intend to take another 3% or so secretly. I want to roll many of the lavish personal expenses I have, including my jet and yacht, into the fees I charge clients. I want all the money the client invests with me to be wired offshore—into an account I've established in the Caymans to avoid paying US taxes. I do not want to have to provide any financial statements or audits by independent certified public accountants to clients. I'm really looking for clients who are willing to let me create rosy valuations for the underlying companies in which I invest client money. And I want clients who are likely to accept my claims of "great performance" without any verification by an independent third party. Maybe I'm asking for too much....

Marketing Consultant: You're not and I have the perfect prospects for you—public pension plans established for state, city, county, and other local government workers and funded by taxpayers.

Mr. Wall Street: Why state government funds? I've had bad experiences with the federal government—the IRS and the SEC. I want to steer clear of government entanglements.

Marketing Consultant: State and local governments that run pensions have long been exempt from almost all federal oversight. Most important, unlike corporate pensions you may be familiar with, they are exempt from federal pension regulations (ERISA). IRS oversight is minimal-to-nonexistent and even when investment scandals arise, the SEC is wary of getting involved in state and local matters that are likely to be highly political. So there's no need to worry about the feds—they ignore, want nothing to do with the trillions sitting in these funds. Likewise, the state and local funds are generally unaware of, and don't care a damn about, fines and disciplinary actions taken by the feds against firms like yours.

And state laws governing these pensions are virtually nonexistent. No worries here.

Mr. Wall Street: That all sounds great but what about state regulators like attorneys general?

Marketing Consultant: Most AGs and other state regulators are elected officials who need to raise money to get reelected and can easily be swayed to look the other way when Wall Street is involved. The last thing they want to do is accuse other elected officials—possibly in their own political party—of stealing from pensions. Pension theft cases are hard to win to begin with, when you add in the politics, no AG will prosecute.

Mr. Wall Street: That's good news. But aren't these state government contracts subject to competitive bidding in Requests for Proposals (RFPs) and lots of disclosures? That is way too much transparency for me. I prefer to work under the radar—in the shadows.

Marketing Consultant: Competitive bidding and RFPs may be commonplace in the federal government contracting world but with the right lobbyists, you can avoid this annoying process with state and local governments. With secret no-bid contracts you can hide all your excessive fees and outlandish expenses, disavow all fiduciary duties as you engage in criminal conduct, and even park the pension cash in the Cayman Islands far from American legal safeguards. The key is identifying precisely what you want to get away with and building it into your contracts. The lugnuts at the pension will sign whatever you give them—they're clueless.

Mr. Wall Street: Aren't there Freedom of Information Act or access to public records laws in every state that would let these secret dealings get out? Isn't the public entitled to know how these public monies are being invested? The last thing I want is to have even a single investor in my fund that might be required to disclose to the world what I'm doing. I'd be screwed!

Marketing Consultant: Not to worry. Over the past decade your colleagues on Wall Street have been working hard to eviscerate public records laws from sea-to-shining-sea. The current ploy is to claim "trade secrets" in your contracts to hide the fees and other scamming. If you grease the right palms with state officials, they will agree to that "trade secret" designation without hesitation. Also, some managers are inserting into their contracts that they will not disclose to the pension any information which the pension may have to disclose to the public under state freedom of information acts. Again, if you know what to ask for—your wishes shall be granted.

Mr. Wall Street: Many of the larger pensions have layers of investment staff—how do I convince them to go along with my scam?

Marketing Consultant: You invite lower-level, less-well-paid pension staff to sit on so-called "Advisory Committees" and lead them to believe this will lead to high-six- and seven-figure Wall Street jobs in the future. Be sure to hold the Committee meetings offshore in exotic locations with lavish meals and entertainment—make staff feel part of the team—and they will look the other way at the high fees, self-valuation, and other bad behavior.

Mr. Wall Street: How do I pay off politicians and other decision-makers without getting caught?

Marketing Consultant: We used to have middlemen called placement agents who would place your bets (bribes) for you, but now thanks to the corporate-friendly United States Supreme Court we have the Citizens United decision which allows almost unlimited secret donations called "Dark Money." Most governors, mayors, political parties, and caucuses for legislators, as well as unions, have Dark Money vehicles that can be used to ensure their cooperation and support.

Mr. Wall Street: I've heard stories about pension plans where the board members like lots of entertainment—i.e., strippers, drugs, expensive meals, and fine wines. Should I anticipate spending big on these items?

Marketing Consultant: Well, naturally, keeping clients happy is never a bad idea—as long as you and your clients are discreet. Go offshore or thousands of miles from home to help avoid any embarrassments. Many times, this helps make the sale. Nevertheless, entertainment—no matter how luxuriant—will almost certainly be a minor expense compared to the bigger Dark Money costs.

Mr. Wall Street: I have to be frank with you. The prodigious fees and expenses I charge to clients will probably make my investment performance uncompetitive, at best. There are certainly better-performing investments out there. How will I keep the business? How performance-sensitive are these funds?

Marketing Consultant: You have absolutely no reason to worry about poor performance. Fortunately, public pensions have no problem with private equity managers like you valuing the underlying companies in which you invest by yourself without any independent third-party verification. So, your performance should always be great. The performance is whatever you tell them it is. As long as the pension staff and any consultants they employ have no access to the underlying assets—as long as you keep them in the dark about the portfolio—they couldn't dispute your self-serving valuations if they wanted to. And trust me, they don't want to. They have much more to lose from full transparency than telling on you. You can sleep soundly knowing that whatever crooked deal they agree to with you, you're not alone. There are plenty of other Wall Streeters feeding at the trough.

Mr. Wall Street: I'm sold! Let's get some of that dumb money!

22

CREATE A BINDING CRADLE-TO-GRAVE ABUSIVE RELATIONSHIP

An experienced, highly successful money management marketer once told me, "The business of managing other people's money is like driving a taxi. The goal is to keep the passenger in the car as long as possible...with the meter running."

So, you've not only got to convince people to willingly hand over their money to you, you've got to persuade them to leave it long enough for you to gradually—imperceptibly—take enough of it for yourself. Transferring their wealth to you is the goal.

The longer you've got their dough, the less you pilfer at any one time, the more likely you'll be free to enjoy spending it. Remember—jail vs. Vail.

There are two basic approaches to locking-in the investor, i.e., maintaining the abusive relationship.

The first is more labor intensive and focuses on the ongoing personal relationship. You must schmooze, wine, dine, and forever cater to the investor's peccadilloes. You make and keep him, liking you. As long as he likes you and stays in your fund, the skimming goes on.

The second approach is far easier and virtually iron-clad. Have your lawyer include in the agreement you give investors to sign, a legal provision which includes—in small print way back in the document—language which obligates the investor for potentially decades to leave his money with you. The beauty of the legal approach is it doesn't matter if, over the passing years, the investor likes or hates you. Whether your performance sucks or not—he's stuck with you. No divorce allowed.

Private equity funds today have the longest commitment periods. Most are sold with an initial ten-year term with up to two, one-year extensions at the discretion of the manager. This suggests a fund term of ten to twelve years. However, most funds exist for much longer than twelve years.

Worse still for investors (but better for scammers), the life cycle of a fund (from inception to final liquidation) is growing longer. For early-stage venture strategies, it is not uncommon to see funds that are fifteen to twenty years old. I've seen private equity funds that bind investors for up to fifty years—virtually from cradle-to-grave. Contracts that do not expressly state a maximum duration may bind investors even longer than fifty years!

So, the key is to get the money in the door, lock the door, and keep it shut! Remember there are no legal limits on how long you can force investors to keep their money with you.

As I detailed earlier, my disciple Duncan—remember Duncan?—after successfully raising $10 million from investors could, twenty years later, end up with $50 million in his pocket… if the passengers stay in his taxi.

> The business of managing other people's money is like driving a taxi. The goal is to keep the passenger in the car as long as possible…with the meter running.

23

SET THE LOWEST POSSIBLE
STANDARDS FOR YOURSELF

Investment professionals are held to a certain "standard of care" under the law. You should familiarize yourself with these standards so you can speak knowledgeably and reassuringly about them to your clients. Do everything you can to ensure that: (1) investors believe you will adhere to the highest standards of integrity; and (2) that the standard of care actually applicable to you is as low as possible. This is what Wall Street does best: tell investors their best interest always comes first, even as every relationship and transaction is structured to benefit the firm at the expense of investors.

"Standard of Care" for Investment Professionals

"Standard of care" refers to the degree of watchfulness, attentiveness, caution, and prudence that a reasonable person in the circumstances would exercise. Failure to meet the standard is negligence, and the professional who fails to meet the standard is liable for any damages caused by this negligence. The standard is not subject to a precise definition and is judged on a case-by-case basis.

For investment professionals, there are applicable securities, investment advisor and trust laws, and regulations which define the standards of care, based upon the nature of the relationship between the parties and the type of services provided.

The relationship between investment professional and client typically involves a high degree of "trust and confidence" because the investor is entrusting the professional with his money. As a result, these professionals are held to heightened standards of care under the law.

Investment advisors are bound to a *fiduciary standard* of care which requires them to put their client's interests above their own. Conflicts of interest must be disclosed and self-dealing is generally prohibited. Brokers are subject to a lower *suitability standard*, which means the broker has to reasonably believe that any recommendations made are suitable for the client, in terms of the client's financial needs, objectives, and unique circumstances. Conflicts of interest and self-dealing are not prohibited.

Virtually all Wall Street firms, in marketing their products, imply or promise they will adhere to the highest standard of care—the fiduciary standard. Think about it: what firm is going to say openly that it will not act solely in the best interest of its clients or put its client's interests first? "We roundly hose our clients," is hardly effective marketing.

When accused of wrongdoing, these same Wall Street firms will defend themselves saying the lowest possible standard of care applies to them.

HOW LOW CAN YOU GO?

For example, in 2015, the Public Investors Arbitration Bar Association, a group of lawyers which represent aggrieved investors, issued a report warning that nine of the nation's top brokerage firms advertise in public as though they are trusted fiduciaries acting in the best interest of investors and then deny in non-public arbitration cases that they have any such duty to avoid conflicts of interest. The group concluded that conflicted advice costs US investors $17 billion a year.[28]

A co-author of the report stated:

"Investors believe they are doing business with individuals they can trust, because the brokers use titles which imply trust, their advertisements give the impression they can be trusted, and the brokers say they can be trusted to look out for the best interests of their clients. A survey of the major brokerage firms show consistency in the advertising, in the tone they take on their websites, and the impression that they intend to leave on investors. Yet when that trust is breached, a survey of answers filed in arbitrations demonstrate that these same firms disclaim liability when held to account in arbitration, and rely on case law to say no such duty exists. The public face of the firms is that they hold themselves to the highest standards, while the private face of the firms, in the arbitration forum where everything is non-public, is that they are mere order-takers."

Scammers should follow the example of the Wall Street crowd and make sweeping promises of undying, everlasting devotion to clients in advertisements and communications. Yet, as is common throughout the investment industry, feel free to ignore those promises made as you steal and disavow them outright should you be challenged.

Your despicable actions will neither surprise, nor alarm anyone. It's simply how the game is played.

Further, scammers can take comfort in knowing that captured federal regulators, such as the SEC and Department of Labor, have long resisted consumer demands for heightened industry standards and have sided with the investment industry to keep standards low.

In short, millions of Wall Street professionals are working and lobbying hard to keep the world safe for scammers like you.

---

[28] https://piaba.org/sites/default/files/newsroom/2015-03/PIABA%20 Fiduciary%20Study%20News%20Release.pdf

You and they are brothers of different mothers—no better, nor worse than the other.

> Familiarize yourself with the standards of care common in the industry so you can speak knowledgeably and reassuringly about them to your clients.
>
> Do everything you can to ensure that: (1) investors believe you will adhere to the highest standards of integrity; and (2) that the standard of care actually applicable to you is as low as possible.

24

KEEPING INVESTORS IN THE DARK: "INFORMATIONAL ADVANTAGES" SCAMMERS CAN EXPLOIT

"Informational advantage" is a key investment concept which every successful investment scammer should fully comprehend and exploit. The underlying theory is that if everyone knew everything, there would be no investment opportunities because the stock, bond, and commodity markets would price all investments perfectly. There would be no opportunity to buy an undervalued stock and sell it at a profit after it goes up in price.

However, in our imperfect world and throughout human history, some people know more than others. Having superior information has a very real value. Recognizing where you hold the informational advantage or, better still, knowing how to create, or exploit, an informational advantage is key.

The more people who know less than you do, the greater your opportunity to profit from their ignorance.

There are four ways scammers can create and exploit informational advantages in the investment industry. They are:

1. **Systems of Mass Deception:** These are investment industry databases maintained by governmental organizations

(with information largely input by industry), such as Financial Industry Regulatory Authority's BrokerCheck system and SEC's Investment Adviser Public Disclosure (IAPD) system which are designed to foster investor confidence, as they enable the industry to under-report scheming. In short, these systems, by design, favor Wall Street and harm investors.

It is important to note that over the decades, the SEC has subtly shifted from its traditional role of compelling disclosure in the Dark Ages to, in the Information Age, obstructing efforts to speed and broaden the flow of material information to investors. Today certain industries hide behind the limited disclosure requirements of the federal securities laws as a defense against ever-greater disclosure that technology permits. They provide the public all SEC requires and nothing more—even though vastly superior disclosure is possible. As a result, the Commission is increasingly irrelevant to institutional investors and is of limited utility to retail investors. It is plummeting to the status of the Better Business Bureau, i.e., an organization only the most naive believe protects their interests from unscrupulous players.

Both with respect to receiving information from outsiders and sharing its information with the public, the SEC has largely followed a failed "closed-door" policy (the exception being its newly-created whistleblower program which rewards a handful of outsiders each year for bringing information regarding violations of law to the attention of the agency.) The SEC rejects the notion that, generally speaking, information gathered to protect investors should be provided to investors. Instead the SEC has taken the position that the agency and it alone should be allowed to decide how much of the information companies are required to submit to the SEC, it will share with investors.

Further, the SEC has long argued in court that the findings of its investigations into money management wrongdoing should not be subject to the Freedom of Information Act. Investors who lose everything at a money management firm that the SEC subsequently investigates or even shuts down, are denied access to SEC reports that might enlighten them as to the causes of their losses. Results of the SEC's ongoing investment advisor inspection program—commonly referred to as "deficiency letters" sent by SEC to money managers at the conclusion of examinations which cite any violations the inspectors have noted—have never been made public, despite the fact that these letters contain valuable information regarding money managers' operations and industry norms. Since 95% of all SEC money manager inspections result in a letter from staff noting deficiencies, access to this vast library of letters would provide investors with a far more realistic picture of the industry. Investors would learn that the firms they entrust with their wealth often are noncompliant with the law and are only to be trusted once integrity has been verified.

2. **Secrecy Schemes:** These are schemes to withhold information foisted upon investors by financial scammers that are commonplace and generally acceptable to investors. In other words, the scammer has convinced the investor that secrecy—maintaining an informational *dis*advantage—is good for the investor.

Perhaps the best, i.e., most lucrative, example of a devious secrecy scheme masterfully designed and executed by scammers today involves the private equity industry. Private equity funds are not publicly-traded mutual funds registered with the SEC and offer none of the protections mutual funds provide. When you invest in a SEC registered mutual fund, you can be reasonably certain that you and all other shareholders in the fund will be treated fairly and comparably. All investors in a mutual fund own a proportionate share of the same investment portfolio, and have identical redemption rights, as well as equal access to publicly disseminated information about the fund's investments.

There are no publicly disseminated prospectuses for private equity funds, and their appalling (ever-changing) private offering documents matter-of-factly disclose that different investors in the fund may pay different fees, participate in different investment opportunities, enjoy different rates of return and redemption rights, as well as have varying degrees of access to information about fund investment strategies and portfolio holdings. It is impossible from the offering documents for investors to determine whether they will be treated better or worse than others because the terms of each investor's participation are secret, known only to him.

The most that private equity offering documents disclose is that certain unnamed privileged individuals "may" be treated better than others and that the preferences granted may result in harm to the other investors.

Private equity funds routinely use "side letter" agreements with select investors to grant preferential treatment. It's hardly a secret that these side agreements exist—the practice of entering into them is disclosed in offering documents and is openly discussed throughout the industry. As a result of increasing institutional investor domination of private equity, and the regulation applicable to these investors, it is now standard practice in the industry for each investor to demand its own side letter. As a consequence, there has been a proliferation of the number of side letters being negotiated with investors, as well as the kinds of arrangements and provisions included in them.

The irony of all this frenetic side-dealing is that every investor who has cut a secret deal with a private equity fund has been convinced by the scamming fund manager that the secrecy scheme is in his best interest because he is getting a better deal than the others! Since investors are never permitted to see all the side agreements, there's simply no way they can know for certain they are being treated fairly and, equally important, that the special rights and privileges granted to others are not harming them.

While it is common knowledge that side letters proliferate, the only real secret is how ugly these agreements can actually be.

Most disturbing of all the side letter agreements I've reviewed are those which specifically provide that fees will be waived for, or compensation paid to, investors who agree to remain in a private equity fund, not pursue fraud claims and not tell the other investors about the fraud. That is, investors who are aware of fraud are paid to keep other unsuspecting investors in the dark (as they and the fund manager continue to profit from the fraud) and to not blow the whistle to regulators. I believe such side letter agreements arguably aiding and abetting fraud raise grave regulatory, even criminal concerns and I have made my findings known regulators.

In conclusion, if the largest, supposedly most sophisticated institutional investors in the world can be convinced by the private equity industry that preposterous secrecy schemes permitting every abuse imaginable—including aiding and abetting fraud, are acceptable, then the sky's the limit for scammers.

3. **Cryptic Disclosures:** Commonplace investment industry legalese or "boilerplate" disclosures can be especially valuable to scammers intent upon confusing and misleading investors, as well as mischaracterizing abusive practices. Scammers who take the time to study industry disclosure practices can learn a lot about how to use disclosures to maintain or enhance the informational disadvantage.

4. **Burying Disclosures:** When all else fails—when you cannot withhold damning information about yourself—bury

the incriminating information under a mountain of worthless, boring, distracting data. In my forensic investigations I've learned that too much information can be as unhelpful as too little.

For scammers, understanding how you and other Wall Streeters can create and exploit informational advantages greatly reduces the risk of getting caught. But, as I discuss below, be aware that it is possible (although highly unlikely) investors today may be able to eliminate or narrow some of the informational advantages.

INVESTIGATING FINRA'S SYSTEM OF MASS DECEPTION

Almost twenty years ago, I downloaded and data-mined the system the securities industry maintained to disclose industry wrongdoing to the general public and conducted the first-ever independent analysis of the data. Why did I do this?

Since the dawn of federal regulation of the stock markets and the stockbrokerage industry in the United States (1930s), firms that buy or sell stocks and bonds on behalf of the public have been allowed to self-regulate. Today the self-regulatory, non-governmental organization overseeing individual stockbrokers and the firms that employ them is a private corporation, known as the Financial Industry Regulatory Authority, or FINRA. FINRA is funded primarily by the brokerage firms that are its members and their employees. The federal government agency which acts as the ultimate regulator of the securities industry, including FINRA, is the SEC.

> "It may be said that the idea of self regulation is just a device to avoid regulation."
> John Dickerson, Asst. Secretary of Commerce 1934

Not surprisingly, for decades FINRA has been widely criticized for failing to vigorously enforce the law, inadequately protecting investors, and putting the interests of the securities firms which are its members ahead of investors.

CRUCIAL ROLE STOCKBROKERAGES PLAY

Securities dealers, commonly referred to as stockbrokerages or "broker-dealers" under the securities laws, play a crucial role in America. These financial institutions can be found from Wall Street to the Main Streets and strip malls of every city in the country, offering their investment products and services to the public. Investors today, both retail and institutional, are likely to entrust a significant portion of their assets to brokerages. Investors may maintain a bank checking account for their short-term cash needs and bill paying; however, increasingly any substantial wealth they may have accumulated is invested with a securities dealer. Yet *independent* (vs. industry) information about specific brokers, firms, and the brokerage industry in general has been extremely difficult to obtain.

The industry via FINRA enjoys a great deal of control over the information the public receives and there are very real limits upon how much information the industry wants the public to have about its bad behavior.

Public disclosure of disciplinary information regarding FINRA's membership is required under the federal securities laws, specifically Section 15 of the Securities Exchange Act of 1934. In other words, FINRA's public disclosure database did not spring forth as a good faith offering to the American public by the self-regulator's membership in an environment lacking a statutory duty. It is important to keep this in mind when one considers the amount and nature of information the industry makes available, as well as the efficiency of the public disclosure system.

Today the public disclosure system FINRA maintains for the public to access disciplinary information about its members is called BrokerCheck.[29] Firms are required to report via BrokerCheck information regarding their wrongdoing.

The very fact that most of the information provided to the public via BrokerCheck is input by the firms *themselves* should tell you something.

EXPOSING FINRA UNDERREPORTING OF INDUSTRY WRONGDOING

I felt compelled to investigate the database the securities industry maintained for public disclosure of its members' misdeeds because in my investigations, I regularly found the FINRA disciplinary database was dead wrong.

Unrepentant individuals and firms involved in serial scamming were not properly disclosing their crimes to the public via the industry database and, as a result, the public was getting screwed time and again by the same miscreants.

Not surprising, the goddamn crooks were not doing what the law required—warning the public to stay away from them!

In December 2001, for very little money—approximately $1,000, I hired a computer geek to create a program to download the disciplinary information (i.e., complaints, criminal events, bankruptcies, lawsuits, and regulatory actions) brought against the nation's stockbrokerage firms—information compiled and maintained by the industry itself—in its entirety.

There was no subterfuge here—I, a former SEC attorney, wrote, asked for, and received written permission from FINRA's legal department to do this.

I then analyzed this disciplinary data or history of misdeeds and published an unprecedented independent analysis called The Siedle Directory of Securities Dealers.[30]

---

29   https://brokercheck.finra.org/

30   Here's a link to the lengthy introduction to The Siedle Directory. http://benchmarkalert.com/WIKI%20Brokerage%20Book.pdf

The analysis concluded that industry's public disclosure system was poorly structured and designed to result in massive underreporting of wrongdoing.

As I stated in the Directory:

"Investors should be aware that the majority of the publicly available information regarding brokers and firms has been prepared by the brokers and firms themselves. Thus, brokers and firms may exercise discretion as to whether and when they disclose information to the public and how they characterize the disciplinary matters they disclose. Some firms are more skilled at avoiding embarrassing disclosures than others. For example, by settling or obtaining "expungement" of customer disputes nondisclosure is assured. Finally, given the current regulatory environment, investors should not readily assume they have information regarding all the disciplinary matters related to a firm. As will be explained more fully later, there are simply far too many loopholes in the system at this time to permit investor confidence regarding firm disciplinary histories."

The Directory revealed that *less than 15%* of the criminal and disciplinary histories were properly disclosed.

Perhaps not surprising, FINRA was not happy to learn from *Fortune Magazine* that the launch of The Siedle Directory was wildly successful and to read, in the *Wall Street Journal,* that a major legal publisher had offered me a contract for ongoing annual publication. Control of the damning data was slipping away from the industry's clutches.

The brokerage industry developed sudden-onset amnesia regarding the prior approval it had granted me and threatened to sue. So, I had to go to federal court in 2002[31] to establish my right to publish the data—and lost.

A few years later, facing rapid technological advances, additional legal challenges, and public criticism, FINRA relented. Today, it is my understanding that the private sector is free to download industry data and make it more useful to investors.

---

[31] https://www.leagle.com/decision/20021388248fsupp2d114011281

There are four takeaways from my experience investigating FINRA's System of Mass Deception:

1. For scammers, think of FINRA as an apologetic disciplinarian, willing to let you get away with damn near anything that doesn't blow up to publicly embarrass the self-regulatory organization.

   FINRA wants to help you help yourself to investor money. If you can learn to use government and industry Systems of Mass Deception to your maximum advantage, then you've essentially got the forces of government and the investment industry assisting your scamming. Let these Systems convince investors you are more credible and trustworthy than you really are.

2. For investors, since the securities brokerage industry is allowed to self-regulate—before you do business with a broker, be suspicious, and investigate fully. There is a conflict of interest inherent in self-regulation.

   FINRA is no friend, ally, or advocate of investors. Think of FINRA as the boyfriend who cheats on you—all the time.

3. Since the industry is allowed to maintain and control access to the disciplinary histories of its members, fully expect FINRA data to understate wrongdoing.

4. When you encounter what I call a "System of Mass Deception," like FINRA BrokerCheck, don't be intimidated if the system appears comprehensive and don't readily rely upon it. Either access the underlying data relevant to your inquiry or choose to be empowered and investigate the overall system. Today, investigations that dig deeper are easier and cheaper than ever.

If you can learn to use government and industry Systems of Mass Deception to your maximum advantage, then you've essentially got the forces of government and the investment industry assisting your scamming. Let these Systems convince investors you are more credible and trustworthy than you really are.

EPILOGUE

Nearly ten years have passed since I began writing the How to Steal series of articles in *Forbes* and unintentionally teaching Duncan Wall Street thieving tactics. Duncan recently proudly told me that since inception, his investment fund has grown (largely through attracting new investors from the church and community by word of mouth) and has been returning approximately four percent annually to investors. His investors are happy—satisfied customers. They believe four percent is an acceptable positive rate of return and none of the investors is complaining about having "lost money," he says.

But even Duncan acknowledges that since his fund has under-performed the over fourteen percent S&P 500 return for nearly ten years—a massive ten percent annual underperformance—his clueless investors have, in fact, suffered significant underper-formance losses. They've lost a lot—more money than they've actually earned. Where has most of the ten percent return they lost each year gone?

Straight into Duncan's once-empty pockets.

The fund has paid him over seven percent annually while his investors have only netted (after fees) four percent annually. The lion's share of the investment return related to his clients' money has gone to him, not them. Better still—for Duncan, not his investors—he has been investing the initial three percent placement fee and seven percent hefty fees he collects annually in high-growth technology stocks like Amazon, Facebook, Google, and Netflix, which have returned a staggering nearly thirty-five percent over the past five years, thanks, most recently, to the COVID-19 pandemic. That's a far greater rate of return than he (or I) had ever assumed in crafting the scheme.

Duncan is now a very wealthy man—and just in the nick of time, he admits. Last month Duncan finally confided that when he originally reached out to me, he was reeling from a lifetime of failures.

"After years spent doing 'the right thing'—getting a good education, marriage with children, landing a decent job, and chasing the conventional American Dream—it all fell apart. My wife cheated on me, my marriage ended in divorce (with loss of custody of my children). I was fired from my decent job, and all the schooling I had did not help me at all. I battled dark thoughts of suicide. I began questioning everything I had ever been told about how to achieve success. It seemed I had been lied to—the way things really work had been hidden from me.

I had been living with failure as my constant companion for so many years and my life was getting worse. If I only knew what the super-rich know. But no one would tell me. Why was I being left out of the club? I was starved for success and had nothing left to lose—my relationship with my kids was terrible. I felt horribly guilty I could not be the provider for them I wanted to be. Maybe I could do what the Wall Street pigs do.

Wall Street was making obscene amounts of money—through legally questionable means—but the regulators and law enforcement did nothing to stop the cheating. Could I do something like that and make crazy money, but maybe not be quite as sleazy? Was it possible? I had no mentors to ask and no one I knew had any idea about wheeling and dealing at the big-money level. So I went to Google to find an answer. I needed to swing for the fences for some business…any business…legal or maybe even…illegal."

So, while Duncan's early life in small town Nebraska was nurturing, the multiple mid-life setbacks he suffered had gradually destroyed his confidence in a just and orderly universe, leaving him haunted with feelings of worthlessness and helplessness. Destitute and out of ideas, he was eager to learn the rules of the dirty game he observed so many others playing successfully. He reached out to the only person offering to reveal the secrets of the realm.

To his credit, Duncan did not succumb to feelings of hopelessness and his outreach to me was shrewd. I and I alone, openly offered to teach what he so desperately wanted to learn: How to legally steal a lot of money like the folks on Wall Street. It was rational—you might say a sign of health—that he contacted me.

Duncan has now achieved his ambitious financial goals—thanks to investors who aren't even aware they've been scammed and who still consider him their trusted friend. As we defined it in an earlier chapter, Duncan is a "successful" financial adviser.

He has made himself rich largely at the expense of his investors.

He has broken no laws.

His road to riches is one thousands of others on Wall Street have travelled without fear of prosecution. Having played by the rules of Wall Street, he can go to Vail, no worries of jail. Duncan also has garnered the respect of his community—even though he and I both know he is not truly deserving of their admiration. Remarkably, his reputation as a successful businessman is so solid that he is considering using some of his wealth to run for public office. He can be confident that, like so many other scammers in public office today, voters will never fully understand the illegitimate means he used to get ahead or, even if they do, not really care as long as his scheming paid off and he is rich.

It's been said "America loves a winner," and it's true. Americans love winners because they restore our faith in our peculiar form of capitalism and reassure us that it is possible for the little guy to succeed against daunting odds. And, while most Americans say "success" is more about happiness than power, possessions, or prestige—money and fame are the conspicuous yardsticks we readily rely upon in judging who's "made it."

Like Duncan, we all need to study the art of investment scamming at the highest levels—devious devices related to specific scams as well as systemic fraud involving the world's most respected and trusted financial institutions. Studying stealing will better equip us to protect ourselves and our families from Wall Street thievery, at a minimum. Alternatively, armed with insider knowledge, we may choose to join in the looting and compete with the scammers. Fortunately in the Information Age via the internet there is more information available about investment scamming than ever and the cost of accessing that information is minimal.

But Wall Street, like cockroaches scurrying into the shadows when the lights are turned on, is—more than ever—vigorously using every legal device to fight transparency and concocting ever-more complex (non-KISS) schemes to transfer investor wealth. The thieves are working harder than ever to continue stealing in the Information Age and are successfully using information technology to pilfer more than ever.

They're winning.

The legal and regulatory systems are failing to protect the shrinking savings average workers have accumulated. The deck is stacked against investors.

They are losing.

Financial literacy programs today must teach students about the ugliness they will encounter. As I stated at the outset of this journey, lying, cheating, and stealing are so commonplace in the world of investing that they are **not** the exceptions. Systemic scamming mercilessly overwhelms any so-called rules and devours those who play by them. So, learning "rules" without learning the even greater larcenous "exceptions" makes no sense—it's reckless. Schools and professors who teach the "rules" alone are negligent, in my opinion and put students, at a minimum, at a competitive disadvantage, or, worse still, in harm's way.

For the student of investing, the choice is simple—either study bad behavior and be forewarned, or risk losing everything you own.

But teaching high-level systemic investment scamming is not solely about combating fraud.

It's also about educating the masses regarding tried-and-true schemes to build wealth and transfer the wealth of others. These strategies are generally taught to only the most ambitious, upwardly mobile graduates of elite colleges and inheritors of great wealth. By providing access to high-level information about industry practices involving asset management, venture capital, private equity, and hedge funds, we'll open (what Duncan referred to as) the Wall Street "club" to outsiders. By destroying the Informational Advantage and leveling the playing field, we will discover whether others can compete in this greed marketplace. Is the Wall Street crowd intellectually superior and therefore more entitled to all the riches it can grab—the last cookie? Or can the masses mimic the self-proclaimed Masters of the Universe?

Through bringing new members into the old club, perhaps we'll get really lucky and change how the dirty game is played.

Finally, for investors, it is critical to keep in mind that investing is far more dangerous—riskier—than you have been led to believe by the media, regulators and Wall Street. Since it is much easier to lose money than recover even some of what you have lost, you need to be cautious and protect yourself from investment scammers before you part with a dime.

Contrary to conventional wisdom, most of the people employed in the financial advisory industry are not looking out for their clients' interests—they are diligently working to advance their own. If you entrust another with your money long enough it is inevitable, given human nature, that he or she will eventually succumb to temptation and put some in his or her pockets—through legal or illegal means. Further, the companies financial advisers work for are looking to profit off your hard-earned savings and employee compensation is largely determined by how much of your money ends up in employer coffers. So, you're not worried about just a "few bad apples," you must act under the assumption that *every* financial adviser you encounter is a crook pursuing his own personal financial gain or his employer's.

Be suspicious of what you read and hear from the financial media. Financial reporters are largely unaware of the depths of investment mismanagement and fraud—wrongdoing that can only be uncovered through in-depth forensic investigations undertaken by industry experts. Such investigations, which I call "autopsies," are extremely rare and usually go unreported. After all, the financial press is hugely dependent upon advertising revenue, so there is a limit to how critical of Wall Street the media is likely to be. Advertisers control, or at least influence, most financial reporting.

As we have discussed, regulators have been captured by the financial firms they regulate and much of the information regulators gather regarding industry wrongdoing is withheld from the public—at the industry's behest. Worse still, the public disclosure systems—aka Systems of Mass Deception—regulators maintain to disclose investment and disciplinary information to investors have been compromised. As a result, wrongdoing is far more widespread and severely underreported to the public. Fortunately, SEC and CFTC whistleblower programs now exist to reward insiders for reporting illegalities which will make it slightly—only slightly—harder for regulators to conspire with Wall Street and keep the investing public in the dark.

Remember that scammers are attracted to certain locales (like Florida) and certain venues (charities, country clubs and churches), where you will need to be especially on your guard. Also, keep in mind that scams are often tailored to, or shaped by, the environments or communities where they are foisted. Whenever you learn of an investment scam, ask yourself: What factors spawned the fraud, contributed to its success and eventual demise? Was the fraud complex enough, i.e., non-KISS, to escape prosecution? Could the scam have been executed legally?

Never make the mistake of assuming that someone who is, or appears to be rich, is necessarily a savvy investor or an adviser who has done well by his or her clients. Most likely, he or she is simply skilled at transferring the wealth of clients to him or herself.

Insist on full transparency with respect to all your investments and never accept adviser assurances that secrecy is in your best interests. Refuse to be complicit in the very secrecy schemes that will screw you.

By paying attention to fees and expenses and limiting yourself to low-cost investments, you will avoid many pitfalls. As a general rule, the sketchiest, highest-risk investments charge the highest, most outrageous fees—fess which are rarely fully disclosed.

Likewise, stay far away from investments that lack readily ascertainable market values (hard-to-value assets) since the managers of such assets can be counted on to inflate portfolio values due to the conflict of interest related being compensated on an asset basis—i.e., the higher the values, the more the managers are paid. Funds investing in hard-to-value portfolios may be especially alluring to investors because they often advertise stellar performance results—returns based upon bogus values. Since all hard-to value investment funds limit transparency—if you demand transparency, you should easily avoid these scams.

Again, lack of transparency, inflation of market values and high fees frequently go hand-in-hand.

Whenever an adviser discloses he "may" engage in activity which is not in your best interests, assume he will. Take seriously the disclosures of risks related to so-called "potential" conflicts of interest and avoid conflicts of interest whenever you can. Most often, the conflicts are real—not merely "potential"—as is the harm conflicts inflict upon investors.

While all of the above may seem overwhelming, to end on a positive note, the very fact that you have read this unprecedented book focusing on Wall Street thievery decreases the likelihood that you'll be the next victim of a scammer.

You're already well on your way to enlightened, informed investing.

SUPPLEMENTARY READING MATERIALS

Time to Recall America's Structurally Flawed 401ks

Forbes, September 9, 2020

The great 401k experiment of the past fifty years has failed generations of America's workers. As controversial as that statement may sound, today there is broad consensus 401ks have not, and cannot, provide meaningful retirement security.

Not too long ago, it was heresy to suggest 401ks were fundamentally flawed.

What if financial products, like harmful consumer products, were subject to safety recalls? To stimulate national debate, in 2008 I drafted the "recall notice" below using a children's toy recall issued by the Consumer Product Safety Commission as my template and sent it out as a press release.

No recall by any agency of government ensued following the market meltdown twelve years ago but at least now it is widely acknowledged these savings plans are flawed and have undermined the retirement security of American workers. Since 2008, the industry has been quietly addressing some of the most grievous abuses, without drawing attention to the defects inherent in the mass-marketed 401(k) "product." (Most recently, however, Trump's DOL and SEC have been busy ramping up the fees and risks related to 401ks by permitting private equity in plans.)

I published the recall again in Forbes in September 2010 and also published an extensive research paper, *Secrets of the 401k industry: How Employers and Mutual fund Advisers Prospered as Workers' Dreams of Retirement Security Evaporated*, which documented the unsavory industry practices that played a significant role in creating the defined contribution retirement crisis the nation faces today. The demise of 401ks was no accident and, indeed, was predictable, I wrote.

My research found that 80% of employers believed 401ks were effective in recruiting employees to come work for them but only 13% of employers believed that the 401k plans they offered would provide retirement security for their workers. In other words, employers understood that offering plans that purported to provide for workers' retirement security, without obligating employers to pay retirement benefits, was helpful in building their businesses. However, employers privately acknowledged that these plans were not sufficient to provide for workers' retirement. On the other hand, employers believed that guaranteed retirement income, such as a traditional pension plan, would be far more costly to provide.

So, I asked, "Do employers tell their workers there really is no retirement security provided if they stay in their jobs and thereby risk losing employees to competitors? Or do employers maintain the charade that they offer retirement security? Has your employer told you it is virtually inconceivable that the defined contribution plan he offers will provide sufficient retirement income?"

It's time to stop calling 401ks "retirement" plans and offer workers meaningful alternatives thoughtfully crafted. It's really not hard to improve retirement plans—provided it's not left up to Wall Street to propose solutions.

NEWS from Benchmark Financial Services: 401k Recall

FOR IMMEDIATE RELEASE October 9, 2008 Release #01-008

Recall of Most of Nation's 401k Plans

Benchmark Financial Services, Inc, with anticipated cooperation of the firms referenced below, today announced a voluntary recall of the following consumer products. Consumers should stop using recalled products immediately unless otherwise instructed.

Name of Products: 401k plans; So-called "Retirement" Plans

Units: Trillions in assets

Manufacturers: Financial services firms globally, assisted by employers

Hazard: Consumer will likely incur excessive fees and poor performance resulting in injury to their financial well-being.

Incidents/Injuries: We have received reports from tens of millions of consumers of injury to adults (especially older adults approaching retirement), resulting in anxiety, loss of sleep, housing foreclosures, and postponement of retirement plans. Hazardous effects of these plans are generally irreversible in older adults.

Description: This recall involves a financial product marketed to America's workers (of all ages) which claimed to provide for their "retirement security." While the product may have some value as a savings vehicle, it will almost certainly not provide for financial security in retirement. Statements that the product will provide retirement security are gross misrepresentations which consumers should disregard. Generally, the investment options within the product were sold unaccompanied by the delivery of an owner's manual (a "prospectus") that would have disclosed the risks related to these products. Furthermore, even the prospectuses that related to the investment options falsely represented that they were subject to comprehensive federal regulation that would protect the interests of consumers. In fact, the federal agencies that regulate these products (Securities and Exchange Commission and Department of Labor) have been found to be compromised by conflicts of interest. Employers offering the products (401k plans) to their workers generally failed to educate themselves regarding its properties and failed to offer more viable alternatives for their retirement planning.

Sold at: Financial services firms globally; however, predominantly in the United States to American workers.

Manufactured in: Globally by many of the leading financial services firms.

Remedy: Consumers should immediately take the recalled 401k plan products to their employers or the manufacturers of these products for refund.

Trump DOL Throws 401k Investors to the Wolves

Forbes, June 13, 2020

Trump US Department of Labor watchdogs just opened the door for private equity wolves to sell the highest cost, highest risk, most secretive investments ever devised by Wall Street to 401k plan sponsors. 401k investors will be devoured like lambs to the slaughter.

Last week, the US Department of Labor opened the door for plan sponsors to add private equity funds to their 401(k) plans. That's a huge win for the private equity industry since 401ks hold nearly $9 trillion in assets and a monstrous setback to American workers who invest in 401ks for retirement security.

After over three decades of egregious retail price gouging by mutual fund companies—as to which the DOL turned a blind eye—401k costs have in recent years been trending downward thanks primarily to widespread excessive-fee private class action litigation. Now, if private equity is embraced, 401k costs will skyrocket, risk will dramatically increase, and transparency will plummet.

Bad enough that DOL—the federal agency which is supposed to protect employer-sponsored retirement benefit plans—welcomed the wolves of Wall Street to feast on workers' hard-earned savings, but the explanation the agency provided for its reckless action is perverse.

Ramping up the fees and risks to 401k savers will "overcome the effects the coronavirus had had on our economy" and "level the playing field for ordinary investors" by allowing workers to gamble their limited retirement savings like millionaires who can afford to lose lots.

According to the DOL press release, Chairman of the US Securities and Exchange Commission Jay Clayton commended the Department's efforts "to improve investor choice and investor protection," saying the new guidance, "will provide our long-term Main Street investors with a choice of professionally managed funds that more closely match the diversified public and private market asset allocation strategies pursued by many well-managed pension funds as well as the benefit of selection and monitoring by ERISA fiduciaries."

The chairman of the world's premier securities regulator evidently is unaware a decade-plus of private equity investing by so-called "well-managed" pensions has resulted in increasingly disappointing, not to mention inflated and unauditable performance results. Warren Buffett, arguably the world's most respected investor, recently escalated his criticism of private equity firms.

At last year's Berkshire Hathaway annual meeting Buffett stated, "We have seen a number of proposals from private equity firms where the returns are not calculated in a manner that I would regard as honest... If I were running a pension fund, I would be very careful about what was being offered to me."

Chairman Clayton and DOL may think they know more about the risks and rewards of private equity investing than Buffett.

They don't.

They may believe gambling on private equity is a prudent strategy for recovering pandemic losses.

It isn't.

In my experience investigating over $1 trillion pensions, struggling plans almost always migrate to riskier, costlier investments in their final hours to save themselves—a Hail Mary that, predictably, only hastens their demise. Gambling is no way to improve retirement security.

Private equity improves investor protection? Given that private equity funds lack all of the hallmarks of prudent investments this statement is especially disingenuous.

As I discuss in Who Stole My Pension? private equity funds are the highest cost, highest risk, least transparent, and most illiquid. Their assets are the hardest to value and the easiest to inflate.

I've investigated thousands of these funds and found rampant violations of law.

SEC staff examinations of private equity firms have reportedly found that more than half allocated expenses and collected fees inappropriately and, in some cases, illegally. Why would a retirement plan regulator open the door to an industry which more often than not cheats? Are 401k investors clamoring for private equity and willing to take their chances?

According to EBSA Acting Assistant Secretary Jeanne Klinefelter Wilson, the new guidance "should assure defined contribution plan fiduciaries that private equity may be part of a prudent investment mix and a way to enhance retirement savings and investment security for American workers."

In my thirty-five years of experience, I have never met a defined contribution plan fiduciary who is capable of fully understanding the heightened risks related to private equity investing. For plan fiduciaries who choose to dance with these wolves, prepare to be bitten.

Every Dead, Zombie Teamsters Pension Deserves an Autopsy

Forbes, May 9, 2016

Every death of a pension deserves an autopsy.

When a pension collapses and the retirement benefits promised to thousands, or even hundreds of thousands, of workers are slashed or eliminated, a postmortem examination to discover the cause of death should be demanded. Lives have been traumatized—retirement dreams shattered.

When a pension dies, experts who opined over its lifetime it never would, have some explaining to do.

Every pension death I've witnessed involved multiple experts responsible for monitoring the deceased's "vital signs" i.e., soundness of the plan, including the calculation of future liabilities and assumed rates of return, allocation of assets, and fees paid to investment managers.

The judgments of these so-called experts are rightfully called into question by the unexpected death. To the extent they may have contributed to the demise of the plan, they should be held accountable.

In my experience, having forensically investigated over $1 trillion in retirement plans, pensions don't just implode overnight. There are always warning signs or "red flags" that have been disregarded for decades. Why?

Pension deaths are almost always foreseeable. Likewise, pension deaths are almost always preventable. If not foreseen and prevented, then someone was not doing their job.

However, autopsies almost never follow pension deaths. Indeed, the possibility of a forensic investigation into the causes of a pension death is rarely discussed. The scope of such an investigation, as well as probable cost, is rarely researched.

Generally, all parties responsible—including the Pension Benefit Guaranty Corporation (the federal government agency that protects pensions)—agree there is no need to investigate the causes.

As I said early last week, Wall Street firms earning fat fees for managing pension assets—conflicted investment consultants recommending asset allocations, as well as money managers who pay them for access to pension clients; brokers executing trades; custodian banks; actuaries, and pension boards—all view an inquiry into potential wrongdoing as ill-advised, even dangerous.

On Friday, a plan to slash the pension benefits of the Central State Teamsters Pension Fund was rejected by the Treasury Department. It would have been the first time the federal government permitted cutting current retirees benefits under a new law.

The good news—if you can call it such—is, for now, hundreds of thousands of union workers and retirees will continue to receive the benefits promised.

The pension has not been pronounced dead.

The bad news—it is expected to die within ten years. Call it a Zombie pension because it already lacks the blood needed to keep it alive.

The plan to slash benefits wasn't rejected because the cuts were unnecessary. To the contrary, the government found that the proposed reductions weren't deep enough. Chances are a new proposal with even deeper cuts surfaces soon, after a suitable cooling-off period.

More than ever, I encourage stakeholders in the Central State Teamsters Pension Fund to organize to forensically investigate the causes of the demise of your pension. The bleeding at the pension goes on. There's far more to this nightmarish tragedy than you've been told.

Unless union workers and retirees learn the facts about their pension—better than the opposition—they will continue to negotiate in the dark any future proposed reforms.

Rising Secrecy, Fees, and Theft Make This the Most Dangerous of Times

Forbes, November 5, 2014

Thirty years ago, when I first entered the money management industry as a young attorney in the Division of Investment Management of the Securities and Exchange Commission in Washington—the Division which regulates investment advisers—there were two fundamental assumptions which both regulators and the regulated shared.

First, the industry assured regulators that over time, as a result of economies of scale, breakpoints in investment advisory fee schedules and competition, the fees money managers charged investors would precipitously decline.

In the 1980s, the Commission was justifiably concerned about high fees prevalent in the industry and the windfall managers were enjoying as assets under management skyrocketed—due primarily to the development of IRAs and 401(k)s.

It was understood by all that there were limits on how much advisers could charge and that higher fees would be deemed excessive by the SEC. Fees would go nowhere but down, ensuring a "better deal for investors" promised the industry.

Second, it was obvious to the Commission and industry that the future would bring ever greater disclosure of material financial information to investors.

As more Americans opened brokerage accounts and invested in the stock market and mutual funds, technology in the Information Age would deliver-up more and better disclosure. Advisers offering, and investors accepting, less disclosure was as unimaginable as reverting back to the Stone Age.

My colleagues and I could not have been more wrong in our assumptions about the industry's future.

Like the funny caveman T-shirt showing an ape evolving into an upright man and then devolving to a creature crouched before a computer screen says, "Something Somewhere Went Terribly Wrong."

Money management fees have exponentially grown to unprecedented levels, thanks to the proliferation of alternative investments such as hedge, venture, and private equity funds. While it was assumed decades ago that the public would be unwilling to continue to pay retail fees of even 1%, today many of the largest institutional investors eagerly pay fees of 2% and 20% of gains— a near 400% increase.

Worse still, paying outlandish fees has not improved net investment performance.

Forget the old adage, "You get what you pay for." In the money management industry, the cheapest passive funds have trounced the vast majority of active managers. Yet many so-called "sophisticated investors" don't even bother to attempt to negotiate fees with their alternative investment managers.

Perhaps most perplexing, investors in alternative funds today are willing to forgo disclosure of any material investment information, as well as consent to outrageous self-dealing and obviously abusive practices.

Alternative investment offerings commonly dictate that the manager has the right to withhold any and all information, or to provide certain investors with enhanced disclosure that can be used to profit at the expense of other clueless investors.

Why any investor would agree to let an unknown insider pick his pocket is beyond my comprehension. Yet dozens of public pension fiduciaries like the Illinois Teachers' Retirement System, Illinois State Board of Investment, San Francisco City and County Employees' Retirement System, Massachusetts Pension Reserves Investment Management Board, Louisiana State Employees' Retirement System, Minnesota State Board of Investment, New York State Teachers' Retirement System, New Mexico Public Employees' Retirement System, Pennsylvania State Employees' Retirement System, and the Washington State Investment Board have agreed to such blatantly unfair treatment.

Managers reserve the right to withhold from investors any information that may negatively impact their reputations, including criminal activity.

Disclosure like the Madoff feeder-funds' explicit warning, "the manager could abscond with the assets," no longer seems outrageous. As long as clients consent to thievery obliquely disclosed, details of the theft can be withheld, and the crime will never be detected or prosecuted.

In short, this is the most dangerous time since inception of the federal and state securities laws to invest. The laws enacted to protect investors have been largely eviscerated by some of the most highly-compensated, ethically-challenged, and politically-influential asset managers in history.

More money than ever is captured in high-risk, high-cost, secretive, fraud-ridden investments.

The public cannot know the related risks to the broad market because these most dangerous investments are not publicly offered with attendant disclosure. Investors in these funds, having agreed to the withholding of any material financial information, have no idea what's going on with their money. Regulators are looking the other way or, at best, issuing vague public warnings of pervasive wrongdoing without identifying the parties involved.

For example, the SEC recently publicly announced findings of bogus fees and expenses at over half the private equity firms the staff reviewed, as well as cherry-picking related to performance reporting and valuation of investments.

Thanks for the tip, SEC—now do something about it.

For investors who ignore the allure of alternative investment weapons of financial destruction and stick with low cost, highly liquid, fully transparent, SEC registered funds, the risks are reduced.

However, don't kid yourself—the secrecy and egregious practices involving trillions of dollars invested in alternative investments is unprecedented. Sooner rather than later you're going to hear about, as well as potentially feel the impact of this scamming forty times greater than Madoff. There will be blood.

Hedge Fund Marketers Flout Country Club Rules

Forbes, July 5, 2011

Recently I got a call from a New York hedge fund manager that needed advice on marketing his fund to pensions.

During the course of the conversation he said, "I see you live in Palm Beach County, Florida. Do you belong to the Sea Dunes (fictitious name) Club?"

I explained that although I lived near the club, I was not a member. "People in our neighborhood who live near the beach often don't belong to beach clubs," I commented. "We tend to have our own pools and beaches. Most members of beach clubs live in-land, away from the ocean."

"Oh, you really should join," the hedgie said, "it's a great place to meet people."

The club in question is a small, private club with an attractive pool, dining, and tennis facilities. It isn't fancy or elaborate and I wouldn't expect any financial titan up north to know about it. On the other hand, it's one of South Florida's older private clubs and has a reputation for old-money members.

What puzzled me was why a New York hedge fund manager would belong to this small club in Florida—one among dozens of others dotting the South Florida coastline. "You must own a home in Palm Beach or nearby," I said answering the question in my mind.

"No, not at all. I stay at the Breakers whenever I go down to Florida," I was told.

This really didn't make sense—belonging to a club thousands of miles away that requires staying at a pricey hotel miles away from the club to even use. That's a high price for a BLT served poolside.

Upon further discussion, it turned out the money manager belonged to the club to meet with clients and, well, market his hedge fund to other members. The arrangement made perfect sense from a business perspective, even though it was impractical on a personal level.

More recently my wife and I were invited by the club to a social gathering for potential new members. It was a bit stuffy for our tastes but pleasant overall and we figured membership was worth considering. Upon request, we were provided with a membership application to complete. The detailed personal information required in the application was pretty daunting. At my age, does anyone really care where I went to high school? (If you do, see my profile on Forbes.com.) But here's where the story gets interesting.

The application stated that the club could not be used to conduct business and members had to attest that they were not deducting their membership dues as a business expense. I'm thinking: How can they monitor compliance with this policy? Do they ask to see tax returns? Yikes! That would be really invasive.

Don't get me wrong. In this post-Madoff age, I'm all for private clubs getting serious about protecting their members from investment solicitations.

More often than you might think, investigations of investment scamming today involve prominent individuals and families. Bernie Madoff was no thug who robbed victims in back alleys in bad neighborhoods; hedge fund scams are generally perpetrated by socially prominent individuals in attractive, exclusive environments where high net worth individuals congregate.

As a result, in these social settings investors should most be on their guard. Hedge fund marketing is, first and foremost, social networking. Due diligence in these circles amounts to little more than asking a friend (who may be even more clueless) for a reference regarding the investment opportunity.

Non-solicitation or no business policies are just fine with me partially for selfish reasons. As a financial investigator I don't want investment scammers to be members of any club I belong to. Having drinks poolside with someone I have investigated or otherwise have reason to believe is involved in wrongdoing isn't my idea of fun.

How hard is it for private clubs to monitor member-to-member investment solicitations? Not very. Many likely violators seem pretty simple to spot. While I may be referred to at Forbes as a "financial watchdog," it doesn't seem to me that you have to be a sleuth to figure out when investment guys from distant states with no local residences are using your private club to trawl for customers.

The tougher issue for private clubs is what to do when prominent members are involved in violations of the rules? I suspect clubs that have such laudable policies rarely enforce them—at least until it's too late. (Bernie, no doubt, at this point in time has been tossed from any private club he used to belong to.) It's challenging to confront members on these issues.

I do strongly object when private clubs that have adopted "no-business" policies allow investment promoters, at least those of certain stature, to flout the rules. Either have rules and enforce them or don't have them at all.

Don't pretend to be high integrity when you're only high net worth.

We never got around to applying to join the private club in question because it was more effort than it was worth to us at the time. The fact that I have investigated some of its longstanding members was an issue but not determinative.

In my opinion, every private club should wrestle with the issue of investment marketing in its midst and develop some response. Private clubs that have policies regarding solicitation should be commended; however, having a policy that is not enforced or only selectively enforced may be misleading to members who are complacent. The Madoff tragedy revealed the dangers related to marketing hedge fund investments to high-net-worth individuals in exclusive social settings.

As hedge funds proliferate, appropriate behavior in private clubs needs to be redefined.

Your State Pension Is Being Robbed

Forbes, July 22, 2020

Expert forensic investigations reveal stealing from state pensions may be rampant, undermining the retirement security of workers. That's an inconvenient truth that neither the inexperienced board of directors overseeing your pension nor the Wall Streeters robbing it want you to know.

Over the past thirty-five years, I have conducted forensic investigations of $1 trillion-plus in retirement plans, including many state pensions.

That's more investigations of pensions than any forensics expert in the world.

In case you're not familiar with my work, I am a former SEC attorney who in 2018 secured the largest CFTC whistleblower award in history and in 2017 secured the largest SEC whistleblower award, both related to a $367 million JP Morgan Chase settlement. In 2016, I obtained the first whistleblower award from the State of Indiana. So, hopefully you'll agree at least these federal regulators believe my insights on potential illegalities are worth listening to, as well as paying for.

Every state pension investigation I've undertaken has uncovered, documented, and reported to regulators and law enforcement myriad forms of widespread industry wrongdoing amounting to billions.

The culprits frequently are Wall Street money managers, investment consultants, lawyers, brokers, and custodian banks. The victims—pension stakeholders—including taxpayers who contribute to these plans and state workers who are counting on them in retirement, are paying the price. If you are a state worker, Wall Street wrongdoing may be undermining your already precarious retirement security.

What types of thievery am I talking about?

In my forensic investigations I have often, but not exclusively, focused upon state pension gambling on the highest cost, highest risk, least transparent investments ever devised by Wall Street—so-called "alternative" investments such as speculative hedge and private equity funds. For over a decade, I have researched alternative investment industry practices and concluded that state pension boards have granted these "lightly regulated" funds "licenses to steal."

Many state pensions are risking 25-50% of their assets in secretive "black box" alternative funds. If you think your state pension is not heavily invested in high-risk alternatives, think again.

In my investigations I have found the true percentages of state pension alternative holdings are, more often than not, misrepresented—i.e., understated—in the publicly available financial statements. The investment performance disclosed in recent years related to hedge and private equity funds has been ugly and the final results are likely to be far worse, in my opinion.

But poor performance based upon inflated, impossible to verify asset values is just the tip of the iceberg.

In a leaked intelligence bulletin published recently, the FBI wrote that it has high confidence that hostile foreign powers and criminals could use hedge and private equity funds "to launder money, circumventing traditional anti-money laundering programs."

The FBI has noted that law enforcement and regulators are not equipped to investigate money laundering at the non-traditional asset managers.

If law enforcement and regulators are not up to the task of ferreting out criminal money laundering, what are the chances your state pension is?

There is not a single state pension in the nation that fully understands the unique risks related to alternative investments and is capable safeguarding workers' retirement funds from the dangers. And money laundering by hostile foreign powers and criminals is only one example of Wall Street exposing state pensions to unacceptable risks. All state pensions and their millions of participants are potential victims due to the lack of meaningful oversight.

As I explain in *Who Stole My Pension?* state pensions are overseen by boards of directors or trustees comprised of lay men and women who generally lack any knowledge or expertise in investment matters. There are a few state and local laws which require one or more board members of public pensions to possess some financial experience but such requirements are extremely rare.

Typically, public pension boards include some individuals, such as active or retired teachers, cops, firefighters, and sanitation workers, who are supposed to (and, in my experience, rarely do) represent the interests of workers and pensioners. Other board members are appointed by politicians, such governors and mayors who are supposed to (and, in my experience, rarely do) represent the interests of voters, aka taxpayers.

Again, typically none of the worker or political representatives on state pension boards know anything about investing—yet they decide how trillions in public pension assets are invested.

What could possibly go wrong, you might ask?

Everything and far more than you can imagine, I have observed.

Given that state pension boards and staff are incapable of protecting assets in high-risk alternative funds, you might think that they would welcome, if not seek out knowledgeable experts. In my experience, state pension boards, at best, ignore leading experts and more often than not respond hostilely when confronted with damning information which conflicts with self-serving recommendations from Wall Street intended to increase the fees pensions pay.

The greater the fees an investment pays to Wall Street, the greater the marketing effort by Wall Street to sell that investment and the more likely state pensions will end up owning that high-cost product, i.e., get fleeced.

Wall Street's solution to every pension problem is and will always be, "pay us more in fees."

With respect to hedge funds, over a decade ago Warren Buffett, the world's greatest investor warned state pensions against these speculative investments. Buffett also very publicly wagered $1 million that hedge funds would not beat the S&P 500 over the next ten years. His pick, the S&P 500 gained 125.8% over ten years. The five hedge funds, picked by a firm called Protégé Partners, added an average of about 36%.

John Bogle, Founder of the Vanguard Group, in a 2013 Letter to the Editor of the Wall Street Journal also warned public pensions that "hedge funds are hardly a panacea."

America's state pensions ignored Buffett and Bogle's expert advice, resulting in hundreds of billions in foreseeable, and indeed foreseen, hedge fund losses. Wall Street, on the other hand, profited handsomely from the exponentially greater fees these funds charge—2% of assets under management and 20 of profits—fees which Buffett regards as "obscene."

Buffett also warned pensions against investing in private equity.

"We have seen a number of proposals from private equity funds where the returns are really not calculated in a manner that I would regard as honest," Buffet said at Berkshire Hathaway's annual meeting in May 2019. "If I were running a pension fund, I would be very careful about what was being offered to me."

Again, Buffett's advice has been almost universally ignored in America. Sadly, foreign pensions are now loading up on the same private equity and other toxic investments Made In America that have failed spectacularly in the USA. America remains the global leader in manufacturing and exporting toxic investments.

Buffett has a consistent history of blasting Wall Street firms for charging high fees for actively managed investments and has recommended pensions invest in low-cost passively managed index funds.

You might think that underfunded pensions struggling to pay benefits would heed Buffett's advice and seek to cut the fees they pay Wall Street.

Embrace austerity. Tighten their belts. Trim the fat.

In fact, every forensic investigation I've ever undertaken has exposed that the nearer a pension is to insolvency, the higher the fees and the greater the risks the pension takes on.

Desperate measures—Hail Mary passes—are resorted to at desperate times.

In summary, ignoring Buffett's advice and choosing instead to follow what I call "gross malpractice generally practiced," translates to pensions:

Using overly optimistic investment return assumptions;

Gambling in high-cost, high-risk hedge and private equity investments;

Paying exponentially greater "obscene" fees to Wall Street;

Entrusting assets to firms that Buffett regards as dishonest;

Eschewing the lowest cost, passively managed investments; and

Moving farther and farther away from transparency.

Again, in my opinion there is not a single state pension board that is competently safeguarding the pension assets it oversees. These lay boards are simply relying upon corrupt advice from Wall Street and ignoring expert opinions which conflict with Wall Street's agenda.

To protect your retirement security, you need to get involved in overseeing your state pension. Do not assume for a minute that someone else is doing that job for you.

How to Steal A Lot of Money from CalPERS, The Nation's Largest Public Pension

Forbes, May 24, 2017

How hard would it be to steal millions from CalPERS, the nation's largest public pension with $320 billion in assets? Easy-peasy.

Yesterday the Wall Street Journal reported a disturbing fact—a fact well known to pension insiders for years. That is, officials at CalPERS do not know the full extent of the fees the pension's private equity managers take out of the pension.

At a 2015 meeting, the chief operating investment officer openly acknowledged that no one knew the performance fees paid.

Let's clarify what's going on here. Presumably the mega-pension knows, or can readily establish, all the fees—asset-based and performance—it pays its money managers pursuant to fee invoices. (A breakdown of other operational fees—which can be significant—can either be gleaned from investment fund financial statements or specifically requested from managers.)

What CalPERS doesn't know is the performance and other fees its managers take directly from the funds they manage for CalPERS without asking, disclosing, or invoicing.

At the same 2015 meeting, the chief operating investment officer admitted, "We can't track it today."

CalPERS claims to have turned to "big data" computer models—algorithms—to understand private equity costs. Supposedly, a software program developed by outside firms determined at the end of 2015 that the pension paid $3.4 billion in performance fees over the past quarter-century to private-equity firms. In 2016, that number was said to be $490 million. Don't believe these figures for a second.

For those who are impressed by opaque algorithms no one understands and that lack effective feedback loops to highlight deficiencies and errors, I suggest reading Cathy O'Neil's new book, Weapons of Math Destruction.

As an expert in ferreting-out hidden, excessive, and illegal investment fees, I would never recommend any pension fiduciary (and certainly not a fiduciary overseeing hundreds of billions in government workers' retirement savings) rely upon an ill-defined computer model to catch criminals.

So, to re-cap the problem facing CalPERS: Private equity managers are taking billions from the pension but the pension has no idea how much. How comforting is that to pension stakeholders? You'd think that California's largest state employee union, SEIU Local 1000 and AFSCME would be concerned about protecting the retirement assets of their members that are participants in the state pension.

Of course, if CalPERS doesn't know how much money these private equity managers are taking out of the pension, it cannot possibly know whether the amounts taken are legitimate or wrongful—i.e., theft.

In my opinion (and based upon my experience conducting over $1 trillion of pension investigations), it is almost certain some CalPERS private equity managers are, shall we say, misappropriating assets from the retirement system. Recent SEC staff findings confirm my views.

In 2014, SEC staff found that more than half of about 400 private-equity firms it examined had charged unjustified fees and expenses without notifying investors. To be sure, CalPERS conceivably could have adroitly avoided the hoards of private equity wrongdoers but, based upon my knowledge of longstanding CalPERS due diligence lapses and monitoring weaknesses, don't count on it. As I wrote in 2011, CalPERS involvement in an investment scheme is no assurance of integrity, or a "Good Housekeeping Seal of Approval."

CalPERS board member JJ Jelincic, who raised the issue of undisclosed fees in the 2015 board meeting mentioned earlier agrees. "We don't know what fees our private equity managers are taking out of the pension and so we can't possibly know whether all the fees are legitimate. When I've raised the issue, I've been told the managers are our 'partners' in the funds and we should just trust them."

I posed the following question to CalPERS today in an email: If CalPERS does not know precisely how much money private equity managers are receiving related to fund assets, how can stakeholders be assured that these managers are not wrongfully taking from the pension?

In response CalPERS said, "Our Private Equity fees are fully disclosed in our Comprehensive Annual Financial Report and in the Private Equity Annual Program Review." In my experience dealing with CalPERS, the board regularly claims certainty as to matters which it barely grasps.

How long has CalPERS known about potential theft by its managers? At least four years.

On March 22, 2013, I sent a letter to the CalPERS board reciting my credentials (for those board members who did not already know me) and emphatically stating, "It is apparent to me, even from a distance that the fund continues to lack many of the safeguards I would recommend to improve management and performance." I received no response to the letter.

A few months later, on May 13, 2013, I sent a second letter to board member Jelincic, as requested, providing further detail regarding issues which in my expert opinion should be investigated fully by the pension. Included in these issues were specifically "undisclosed fees related to investment providers/vendors," and "private equity and hedge fund conflicts of interest, fee abuses, and malfeasance."

I am told that when Mr. Jelincic brought my second letter to the attention of the board at a closed meeting, the Board President responded, "How is this letter different from any of the thousands of others we receive?" The suggestion to meet with me was rejected, I am told by Jeincic. CalPERS today stated, "We cannot comment on issues that are discussed in closed session." (Please see update at the bottom of this article.)

If it's true that the CalPERS board regularly receives thousands of letters from forensic experts and other credible whistleblowers alleging potential wrongdoing regarding pension investments—allegations of wrongdoing which the board routinely ignores—that's really scary. Unions protecting government workers should be alarmed that such warnings go unheeded and demand to see all such correspondence.

My advice to would-be criminals: If you want to steal millions, escape detection and prosecution, then set your sights on the mother of all pension honey-pots, CalPERS.

Billions for Bupkis: Pension Placement Agents

Forbes, June 25, 2014

Forget the old adage, "work smarter, not harder." A decade ago, the savviest Wall Streeters discovered a way to make millions doing no work at all.

You can't "work" any smarter than that in my book.

Not surprising, these effortless riches schemes emerged in the surreal land of public pensions—skimming from the trillions in retirement funds set aside for state and local government workers—and, once devised, were shrouded in secrecy.

If the chance to make millions for doing little or nothing is appealing to you, it's not too late to get in on the action. Anyone can become a so-called pension placement agent—no investment experience or education is required.

For example, with respect to a placement agent hired by real estate money manager, C.B. Richard Ellis, a recent review conducted by North Carolina State Treasurer Janet Cowell stated, "The review uncovered no evidence that Dworsky (the placement agent) had any subject-matter expertise regarding the investments being sold by CBRE or the particular investment needs of North Carolina state pension."

No need to apologize for a lack of "subject matter experience" in this biz.

With respect to a placement agent retained by another manager, Avista, the Treasurer's review dryly stated, "Avista did not investigate whether Aqueduct (the placement agent) had a "due diligence committee" or the capacity to conduct due diligence... While it directly retained Aqueduct as its "consultant" and ultimately paid it $1 million for at most a few weeks of work, Avista did not determine whether Aqueduct prepared any due diligence, reports, or analysis, whether it had performed any meaningful work, or whether it shared any information or analysis with the North Carolina state pension."

EDWARD SIEDLE

A million for "at most a few weeks" work that, ahem, may not have been performed. Sweet.

Earlier this month a long overdue ban of placement agents was finally passed by the City of New York pension funds. Don't let that deter you. There's still plenty of money to be made before any effective regulatory response kicks in—if ever.

A Securities and Exchange Commission proposed placement agent ban was defeated by the industry a few years ago and across the nation more public pension money than ever is flowing into the pockets of placement agents.

Here are some of the basics you'll need to know to embark on this career path—assuming getting paid for doing nothing can be called a "career."

A placement agent is an individual or firm hired to act as an intermediary, or middleman for an asset manager, to market and sell its investment products to investors. Placement agents, as "third-party marketers," are not employees of investment managers subject to continuous manager supervision of their activities. As a result, absent full and complete disclosure, investors are often unaware that placement agents are paid marketers for the managers that have retained them and are ignorant regarding the outlandish amounts of compensation they may receive for steering investors.

Placement agent fees are massive in absolute dollar terms, often amounting to millions per institutional investment for only a few hours work.

Further, these avoidable alternative investment marketing fees alone are exponentially greater (ten times or more) than the total fees traditional stock and bond managers charge for actually managing client assets.

As a percentage of the total cost of the management of alternative assets, paying fifty percent to a marketing intermediary is clearly extravagant, in my opinion.

Placement agent fees are generally paid directly by money managers and indirectly by investors through higher asset-based fees than would be available absent the compensation arrangement between the manager and the marketing intermediary. However, placement agent fees may be paid directly by institutional investors.

For example, as reported by Forbes in Ponying Up to Camelot, April 19, 2004, the Chicago Teachers' Pension Fund balked at paying a marketing fee to a firm owned by Edward M. Kennedy Jr.—a fee that the other sixty institutional investors in the fund had paid.

Under the economic theory of disintermediation, removal of the intermediary from the process, i.e., "cutting out the middleman," reduces the cost of the service to the customer. Disintermediation initiated by customers is often the result of high market transparency. Markets lacking transparency often are plagued by undisclosed, dispensable intermediaries.

The Investment Advisers Act of 1940 generally requires that registered investment advisers, when employing the services of third-party marketers, provide the client with a written disclosure document, commonly referred to as a "solicitation agreement," describing the terms of any compensation arrangement between the solicitor (or marketer) and the investment adviser, as well as "the amount, if any, for the cost of obtaining his account the client will be charged in addition to the advisory fee, and the differential, if any, among clients with respect to the amount or level of advisory fees charged by the investment adviser if such differential is attributable to the existence of any arrangement pursuant to which the investment adviser has agreed to compensate the solicitor for soliciting clients for, or referring clients to, the investment adviser."

In summary, the disclosure requirements related to SEC-registered investment advisor third-party solicitation arrangements reflect the belief that the investment advisory client should be advised of the existence of the intermediary, the fees paid to the intermediary, and whether he is paying a higher fee as a result of the intermediary.

In my experience, the SEC has required registered investment managers utilizing undisclosed solicitors to offer public pension investors rescission of the investment (including reimbursement of any investment losses) and return of all fees paid. Thus, failure to disclose marketing intermediaries can have severe consequences for investment managers. The damages in these cases are not limited to the amount of the undisclosed compensation to the intermediary; rather, placement agent fees plus any losses or underperformance may be claimed.

Alternative assets, such as hedge, venture, private equity, and real estate investments, by definition lack the transparency and liquidity of traditional, publicly-traded assets.

The fees charged by investment advisers for managing alternative assets are exponentially higher than traditional asset classes. These outlandish fees enable alternative managers to richly compensate intermediaries who raise capital on their behalf. Since the arrangements alternative asset managers establish with placement agents lack the transparency common to traditional asset accounts, customers are kept in the dark—ignorant of the excessive portion of the investment advisory fee that will be paid to the intermediary for little but marketing to them.

Placement agents are generally compensated by managers based upon a percentage of the amount of capital raised or committed. Compensation is typically between one and two percent of the commitment, but may be substantially greater—three percent or higher, and is usually paid over an agreed upon period of time.

For example, the placement agent fee related to a $200 million investment may be an astronomical $6 million, twenty-five percent, or $1.5 million payable upon closing of the investment, and the remaining balance payable over the next three years—compensation which is obviously wildly disproportionate to any limited marketing services provided over the period.

Because they are compensated in this manner, placement agents are regulated by both the United States Securities and Exchange Commission and the Financial Industry Regulatory Authority.

Since the primary or even exclusive service placement agents provide is introducing investment managers to prospective clients based upon pre-existing relationships, placement agents may utterly lack any relevant financial expertise.

Some placement agents focus exclusively or primarily on a particular type of investor, such as high net worth individuals, institutional investors, or even public pensions. Placement agents focused upon public pensions have established relationships with elected officials and trustees overseeing these assets, including as significant donors to their and allied political campaigns. As a result, use of placement agents in the public pension context is most controversial and potentially dangerous.

Placement agents and the investment managers that retain them maintain that agents provide services of value to institutional investors, such as access to high- demand investment funds, or to minority and women-owned firms; however, the value of such services is, at best, clearly minimal—particularly with respect to larger institutional investors, in my opinion.

Virtually all large public pensions employ one or more investment consultants to recommend managers to be hired and monitor the performance of incumbent investment managers. Investment consultants typically charge large funds far more reasonable fees of less than one basis point—exponentially less than the one to three percent placement agents charge—and the advice they provide is independent—unlike the promotional information placement agents offer.

Institutional investors that retain investment consultants generally seek to avoid use of placement agents due, in part, to the myriad risks involved in including them in the investment decision-making process, such as:

The promotional information provided by these marketing intermediaries lacking investment expertise is, at best, conflicted and unreliable;

Any introductions and meeting facilitation services they may offer are unnecessary;

The exorbitant fees they charge, which bear little relationship to any services actually provided are impossible for well-intentioned fiduciaries to justify as reasonable; and Legal, regulatory, and reputational risk concerns are formidable.

Further, with respect to public pensions in particular, "politicization" of the investment decision-making process whereby hiring decisions are made based upon factors other than the merits of the investments offered, such as the political connections of placement agents that managers have hired to represent them, is yet another reason to forego or prohibit placement agent involvement.

The role and compensation of placement agents related to alternative investments has become a highly controversial issue in recent years as interest in investing in alternatives has grown. As a result of underfunding and stagnant market returns, public pensions, in particular, have significantly increased their allocations to alternative investments. While use of placement agents is not limited to money managers seeking investment from public pensions, revelations regarding "pay to play" schemes involving placement agents related to public funds have been widely reported in Illinois, New York, California, Ohio, and New Mexico.

Due to mounting grave concerns, on August 3, 2009, the SEC issued a proposed rule that would have banned the use of placement agents. While the New York State Comptroller and New York City Comptroller expressed strong support for the ban on using third parties to solicit government plans, most commenters on the SEC proposed rule, including many representing advisers, broker-dealers, placement agents and solicitors, and some government officials, strongly opposed the ban. Facing stiff industry opposition, the final rule adopted by the Commission did not include a ban.

A number of states, such as California, New Mexico, and Illinois, have enacted legislation regulating the use of placement agents and some public funds have adopted policies banning any use placement agents. Most public funds that have adopted placement agent policies require disclosure of certain prescribed information; however, enforcement of these policies has largely been ineffective.

In summary, despite widespread awareness of the proven risks and unjustifiable billions in avoidable costs involved in using placement agents, the industry has successfully resisted efforts to end placement agent abuses related to public funds nationally.

There are still big bucks to be made as a placement agent preying upon public pensions and my advice is to go out there and grab some of it for yourself.

"Work smarter, not harder" is so passé when millions can be made for no work at all.

When Money Managers Get Paid Handsomely for Doing Nothing

Forbes, May 1, 2019

Private equity managers charge fees on committed, uninvested capital because they can.

What's better than getting paid 1% to manage people's money?

Answer: Getting paid 2% to not manage it—for doing nothing.

In certain niches of the money management industry it is common practice for managers to charge fees—typically 2%—on money merely committed to a venture—money the manager does not even manage yet.

This amounts to adding insult to injury since these types of investment funds already charge exponentially higher fees than traditional stock and bond managers.

In 2017, reportedly fees on committed, uninvested capital were the norm in private equity funds. That is, 91% of private equity managers demanded investors pay fees today on money investors had committed to invest over time, say, over the next ten years.

In my opinion, there is no justification for these bogus fees that virtually all private equity managers charge, and investors pay without objection.

When, in my forensic investigations, I bring millions in fees paid on committed, uninvested capital to the attention of supposedly savvy institutional investors (aka fiduciaries overseeing other people's money), initial disbelief and embarrassment swiftly turns to defensiveness.

Overnight, victims and perpetrators agree there's nothing wrong with a failing pension paying even tens of millions to Wall Street for nothing.

Private equity managers charge fees on committed, uninvested capital because they can—because they've convinced investors these funds will produce stellar returns.

An intelligent investor focuses on fees because, unlike performance, fees are the one thing the investor can control.

On the other hand, many so-called "sophisticated" investors don't focus on, or give a damn about, fees. They will pay anything if they believe a money manager is going to make them big money.

Ironically, the more underfunded a pension, the more willing it is to pay outlandish fees—to gamble itself out of a hole.

As we saw in Madoff, many investors, even today, can be persuaded they're lucky to have their money managed by the priciest gunslingers.

So, the lesson is, if a money manager's sales pitch is good enough, he can even get away with outrageously high fees for doing nothing.

The sky's the limit.

Rhode Island Governor Raimondo Redefines Venture Capital Success

Forbes, May, 2016

In 2006, the Employee Retirement System of Rhode Island committed $5 million of worker retirement assets to a small Point Judith II venture capital fund managed by Gina Raimondo—a Rhode Island native who would go on to become, as General Treasurer, the chief fiduciary of the state pension that invested in her fund.

During her first year as Treasurer, she spearheaded a "reform" of the pension which reduced the state's assumed return on pension investments, slashed workers' benefits, exponentially increased fees paid by the pension to Wall Street money managers and resulted in the fund significantly underperforming its peers. By my estimate, Raimondo's tenure cost the pension $1 million a day, or $1.4 billion, in investment underperformance.

In 2014, as a result of the losses she caused to the pension, I suggested that Rhode Islanders should consider paying her to "go away."

Wall Street embraced and touted Raimondo's so-called pension reform nationally and unprecedented amounts of out-of-state money rolled in, supporting her 2014 gubernatorial bid. Raimondo won the race, despite emerging evidence of pension mismanagement.

Based upon performance information disclosed today by the pension, as of six months ago, December 31, 2015, Raimondo's Point Judith II showed an internal rate of return of -1.1%.

That's right: For the past decade, the high-cost, high-risk, opaque Point Judith investment pitched by the governor to the pension has actually lost money.

(As footnoted on the pension's website, the performance calculations are specific to the state's investment and were not prepared, reviewed, or approved by the General Partners. That is, other investors in the fund may have done better—or worse—depending upon the fees and other terms they agreed to.)

Until today, the state pension disclosed private equity performance only through September 30, 2015. Through that date, Point Judith had returned point three (0.3%).

On April 18th, I asked current Treasurer Seth Magaziner to disclose the updated performance of the Point Judith II fund. In response, his Communications Director David Ortiz emailed me, "Because of the illiquid nature of private equity assets there is a quarterly lag between the end of the year and when private equity funds provide their valuations. The calendar-year returns of ERSRI's private equity funds will be available in the April State Investment Commission book, which will be distributed to the board this coming Friday in advance of the board's next meeting on April 27. I can send you the SIC book on Friday once it has been shared with the board."

I repeatedly requested the performance since Friday; today Ortiz finally followed through on his promise.

It seems Raimondo, who Fortune and Institutional Investor credit with reforming (even saving) the state pension when she served as General Treasurer, did the fund no favors when she sold it Point Judith II.

Over the ten-year period through September 30, 2015, the S&P 500 returned 6.8% and even T-Bills earned 1.26%—exponentially greater performance achievable with significantly lower fees and risk.

To be fair, some of the state pension's private equity investments have netted positive results over the past decade (say, 17.5%) or even soared short-term (108%)—Raimondo's did not.

Despite these negative investment results, Raimondo has repeatedly claimed to be a "fortunate and successful" venture capitalist. The firm she started, Point Judith Capital has "flourished in a hugely male-dominated industry," she said in 2010.

In her 2014 "Back To Work" campaign advertisement, Raimondo, then General Treasurer and one of four Democrats running for governor, stated that her former venture capital firm,

Point Judith Capital, helped create more than 1,000 jobs when she was partner.

The ad shows Raimondo at Nabsys, a biomedical company in Providence.

"Before I was State Treasurer, my Rhode Island business helped create over 1,000 jobs, including here at Nabsys, a biomedical company," Raimondo said. "As governor, I'll use this as a model for how we create manufacturing jobs. I'll bring colleges and industry together to develop new products in marine science, green technology, and medical devices, and to train our workers to fill those jobs ... We need to get Rhode Islanders back to work."

It seems Nabsys was no model for job creation.

Nabsys, which received over $40 million—including millions in investment and loans from both Rhode Island's Slater Fund and Raimondo's Point Judith venture fund closed in September 2015 after it failed to find a merger partner or acquirer.

Raimondo's claims of former glory as a venture capitalist, coupled with the closely-guarded performance history of the fund she once managed for the state pension begs the question: What does it mean to be a successful venture capitalist? Is it enough to handsomely profit personally, as Raimondo has? Or is doing well for your clients—such as the state pension you subsequently oversee as General Treasurer aka chief fiduciary—required?

As noted in a recent article in the Providence Journal, the state pension paid approximately $800,000 in investment management fees to Raimondo's venture firm to achieve negative returns. Good for the firm and presumably Gina, not-so-good for workers and retirees.

At the time the pension invested in the Point Judith fund the State Investment Commission had a preference for in-state funds, said Marcia Reback, a longtime member of the Commission and former leader of the Rhode Island Federation of Teachers and Health Professionals to online news GoLocalProv.

Point Judith Capital was the only venture capital fund in the state.

"Point Judith had a leg up," Reback is quoted as saying.

After Raimondo's election, Point Judith Capital relocated to Boston. "At the first opportunity, they moved out of Rhode Island," Reback said.

When the state was later given an opportunity to invest in Point Judith again, Reback told GoLocalProv the Treasurer's staff declined.

As I noted in my 2013 forensic investigation of the pension, «at the time the pension invested $5 million, it appears Point Judith's total assets under management with any investment performance history amounted to, at most, $15 million in a prior Point Judith I fund—a fund which Point Judith Capital had managed for only five years. For a state pension to give a small money manager with a limited track record an amount equal to a third of the manager's total assets under management was a huge leap of faith.»

I also noted, "Not only is Point Judith Capital a small investment firm with limited investment history, it is involved in an industry—venture capital—which is noted for a profound lack of regulation and transparency. Neither the firm nor Raimondo have ever been registered or licensed by the SEC as a securities broker, investment advisory representative, or investment advisor. As a result, key information regarding the partners and the firm, such as assets under management, types of clients, asset based and performance fees, disciplinary information, and marketing arrangements is unknown to regulators and law enforcement, as well as the general public."

In raising money for the fund, Point Judith told investors that the firm had "a strategic partnership with Tudor Investment Corporation" and that, the "lead investor in the fund was Tudor, a preeminent alternative asset management firm with approximately $15 billion in total capital." According to Institutional Investor, Tudor became the lead investor in Point Judith Venture Fund II, with a $15 million commitment and also took an equity stake in Point Judith Capital, the adviser of the fund.

A Power Point presentation by Point Judith Capital to the pension board stated that the terms of the Point Judith II fund provided for a standard fee (2% average) and a carry (20%). Yet, for some reason, the pension agreed to pay a higher fee (2.5 percent) than the fee stated in the presentation (2 percent). Getting a higher fee than you ask for is fortunate indeed—a marketer's dream.

In a letter Treasurer-elect Raimondo wrote to the Rhode Island Ethics Commission seeking a favorable Advisory Opinion regarding her ties to Point Judith, Raimondo represented that the State Investment Commission had entered into a ten-year contract with Point Judith. Approximately ten years later, in response to a recent letter to a retiree inquiring regarding the end date for the Point Judith contract, current Treasurer Seth Magaziner's office stated, "The mandate of the fund is to make a number of investments into private start-up companies which will be sold at a later date for return on capital. As a result, there is no specific end date for our engagement."

Not sure why a fund that makes investments that will be sold at a later date necessarily has no end date. Seems to me most investment funds make investments to be sold at a later date.

Treasurer Magaziner goes on to say, "The terms of the fund are to make investments during a period of six years. After acquiring the investments, the fund manager helps these companies grow and eventually sells the investment, seeking the best return on exiting the investments. These companies will be sold at different times depending on their stage of development.

"Also, market forces may influence the best time to exit—it is better to exit in a strong market when evaluations are high than in a weak market when evaluations are low. We expect that the fund will use its judgment around the time to exit to maximize investor return as opposed to setting a date to exit that may be detrimental to our returns. Exits typically happen between years 8-15. Point Judith has returned $1.9 million of our $5 million invested, and we expect to receive the rest over the next two to three years."

The good news—if it can be called good—is that the state pension, after a decade, has gotten about 40 percent of its high-risk capital back.

Treasurer Magaziner says the governor's former firm—of which the governor is still an owner—has an indefinite number of years after the ten-year investment contract with the state pension terminates before a final reckoning when end performance is calculated.

Governor Raimondo is truly fortunate to have such an understanding pension client.

It seems it will be a while before Gina Raimondo's venture capital investing skills can be definitively determined. However, for over a decade her firm has apparently earned fees of approximately 2.5 percent on an investment that has lost the state pension 1.1 percent.

Better still (for her), Raimondo told the Ethics Commission that she has an illiquid ownership interest in the Point Judith II fund that she received in return for work she previously performed at Point Judith. In other words, unlike the state pension, Raimondo did not pay millions for her interests in the fund. She paid nothing. Whether the investment results she has personally enjoyed related to the fund are the same as the state pension's is unknown. I would think the Rhode Island Ethics Commission would want to know.

If doing well for yourself is the definition of success as a venture capitalist, then Raimondo clearly meets and beats the benchmark—even if she had to, as the chief fiduciary of the state pension, slash workers' cost of living benefits to achieve her personal financial goals.

Trump DOL, SEC Fail to Warn 401ks About Massive Private Equity Dangers

Forbes, August 23, 2020

Trump's US Department of Labor is pushing 401k sponsors to include the highest cost, highest risk, most secretive "private equity" investments ever devised by Wall Street in the retirement plans they offer to America's workers.

Chairman of the US Securities and Exchange Commission Jay Clayton claims including private equity in 401ks will allow workers to choose "professionally managed funds that more closely match the...asset allocation strategies pursued by many well-managed pension funds."

Neither Trump's DOL nor SEC has said a word to 401ks about the massive dangers related to private equity investing.

If you are a corporation that sponsors a 401k retirement plan for your employees or a worker who participates in a 401k, here is a preliminary list of just a few of the myriad dangers you should be aware of—risks which, contrary to SEC Chairman Jay Clayton's naïve comments about "well-managed pensions"—not even the most sophisticated pensions fully understand.

This list is derived from several very public forensic investigations my firm has undertaken involving over $100 billion in pensions—funds in Rhode Island, North Carolina, and New York that lost big gambling in private equity, blithely unaware of the risks. Again, this list of sixteen risks is incomplete—a starter kit for would-be private equity investors.

1. High-risk, speculative investments. Private equity offering documents generally prominently state (in capital, bold letters) that an investment in a private equity fund is speculative, involves a high degree of risk, and is suitable only for persons who are willing and able to assume the risk of losing their entire investment.

If you're comfortable gambling your retirement savings and losing it all, then proceed onto risk #2.

2. High-cost, involving myriad opaque asset-based, performance, and other fees and expenses. Private equity investments charge myriad opaque fees and expenses exponentially (10x) greater than traditional stock and bond funds. You'll never know for sure the total cost of investing in these funds because disclosure of fees and expenses is generally incomplete.

   My investigations often reveal annual fees in excess of 6% for large institutional investors. 401ks will pay even more.

3. Illiquid, lacking a public market. Private equity investments generally do not permit redemptions during the life (generally 10-13 years, but may be as long as 50 years) of these investments. The partnership interests offered are illiquid. No public market for the partnership interests exists and none will be developed. You won't be able to redeem or sell.

4. Lack of transparency. These investments utterly lack a hallmark of prudence—transparency. The information they provide to 401k fiduciaries and other investors is limited, often incomplete and impossible to verify.

   If you're good with putting your retirement savings in a "black box" investment, then proceed by all means.

5. Largely "unconstrained" and may change investment strategies at any time. Private equity funds generally disclose specific risks related to investment strategies they may pursue. However, the managers reserve the right to pursue virtually any investment strategy—at any given time. Thus, it is impossible for investors to know for certain at any given time the composition of a fund's portfolio, the appropriateness of the investments, and the related risks.

   Are you comfortable investing in potentially usurious payday loans to the poor and controversial life settlements purchased from the elderly terminally ill? If so, proceed to #6.

6. Use of leverage. Private equity funds generally reserve the right to engage in borrowing, or leverage, on a moderate or unlimited basis. Leverage increases dramatically the risks related to investing in a fund and the degree of leverage may change at any time.

   You have no control over and will never know the degree of leverage employed at any given time. That's why you could lose everything.

7. No assurance of diversification. Since funds generally reserve the right to invest 100 percent of their assets in a given sector or investment, such as cash, there is no assurance of diversification. How does 100% invested in a single sector, 100% levered sound? Dicey?

8. Lack of comprehensive regulation in the US. Private equity funds are not subject to the same degree of regulation as mutual funds and other US registered funds.

9. Heightened offshore legal, regulatory, operational, and custody risk. Many private equity funds are organized and operate in offshore tax havens, such as in the Cayman Islands, which lack the legal, regulatory, and operational safeguards offered in the US. Also, fund assets may be held, or custodied, offshore. Funds which are incorporated and regulated under the laws of foreign countries present additional, unique risks which 401k fiduciaries and investors should consider. Any problem with having your retirement savings held offshore in the Caymans?

10. Myriad conflicts of interest, self-dealing practices. Private equity funds generally disclosed myriad conflicts of interest involving the investment managers to the funds and others. For example, the investment manager determines the value of the securities held by the fund. Such valuation affects both reported fund performance as well as the calculation of the management fee and any performance

fee payable to the manager. The investment managers are subject to a conflict of interest because they can profit from inflating values. Further, the performance fee structure creates an incentive to the investment manager to engage in speculative investments and thus a potential conflict with the interests of the investors.

11. Business practices that may violate ERISA. Private equity fund offering documents often disclose that investors agree to permit managers to withhold complete and timely disclosure of material information regarding assets in their funds. Further, the fund may have agreed to permit the investment manager to retain absolute discretion to provide certain mystery investors with greater information and the managers are not required to disclose such arrangements. As a result, the fund you invest in is at risk that other unknown investors are profiting at its expense— stealing from you. Finally, the offering documents often warn that the nondisclosure policies may violate applicable laws. That is, certain practices in which the fund's managers engage may be acceptable to high-net-worth individuals (or unknown to them) but violate laws applicable to ERISA plans. Comfy with violations of law in your 401k? Can you ever really be sure your 401k is in compliance with the law when the private equity managers disclose they may not be? Why would Trump's DOL and SEC recommend investments that disclose they may violate the laws of the land?

12. SEC finds pervasive private equity bogus fees and illegalities. A majority of private equity firms inflate fees and expenses charged to companies in which they hold stakes, according to a 2014 internal review by the SEC, raising the prospect of a wave of sanctions against managers (including potentially some of the Fund's private equity managers) by the agency. More than half of about 400 private equity firms that SEC staff examined charged unjustified fees and expenses without notifying investors.

13. Private equity transaction fees securities law violations. Transaction fees charged by private equity funds, sometimes called the "crack cocaine of the private equity industry" because the fees are not traditionally subject to minimum performance requirements, are increasingly opposed by public pensions, and have recently been the subject of an SEC whistleblower complaint filed by a senior private equity insider. The SEC whistleblower credibly alleged that private equity firms have been violating securities laws by charging transaction fees without first registering as broker-dealers with the SEC. If the private equity firms included in your 401k have been violating the state and federal securities laws, they may be required by the states and the SEC to refund to investors the transaction fees wrongfully charged.

14. Private equity monitoring fees tax law violations. With respect to private equity so-called monitoring fees paid by private equity owned portfolio companies, whistleblower claims have been filed with the Internal Revenue Service alleging that these fees are being improperly characterized as tax-deductible business expenses (as opposed to dividends, which are not deductible), costing the federal government hundreds of millions of dollars annually in missed tax revenue.

15. Private equity management fee waivers tax law violations. The IRS has in recent years been examining the propriety of private equity management fees waivers, which have allowed many fund executives to reduce their taxes by converting ordinary fee income into capital gains taxed at substantially lower rates, costing the federal government billions of dollars annually in missed tax revenue. Why would Trump's SEC and DOL recommend investments to 401ks managed by tax dodgers?

16. Private equity under-reporting of massive fees. According to a recent New York Times article, the rates of return and hidden costs related to private equity are difficult for

even investors in these deals to identify. While certain fees associated with private equity funds are widely known—managers typically charge investors 1 to 2 percent of assets and 20 percent of portfolio gains—other charges, including transaction fees, legal costs, taxes, monitoring or oversight fees, and other expenses charged to the portfolio companies held in a fund are less visible—including unauthorized or bogus fees.

According to a 2015 report by CEM Benchmarking, a consulting firm that offers pension fund performance analysis, more than half of private equity costs charged to pension funds is not being disclosed.

(SEC Chairman Jay Clayton apparently is unaware that "well managed" pensions have long been clueless about private equity fees.)

CEM concluded that the difference between what funds reported as expenses and what they actually charged investors averaged at least two percentage points a year. That is, estimated total direct limited partner costs amounted to 3.82 percent. CEM acknowledged this estimate is probably low. A 2007 academic paper found that the average private equity buyout fund charged more than 7 percent in fees each year.

In my forensic investigations of over $1 trillion in retirement plans, I have never encountered a pension that fully understood the dangers of investing in private equity. NEVER. For Trump's DOL and SEC to suggest that 401k sponsors and workers will prosper—recover their COVID-19 losses—through gambling on the highest cost, highest risk, most secretive investments ever devised by Wall Street is ludicrous.

Mourning Vincent "Buddy" Cianci, Rhode Island's Least Dangerous Politician

Forbes, January 29, 2016

I first met Vincent "Buddy" Cianci, the celebrated ex-mayor of Providence who dominated Rhode Island politics for decades, at Tammany Hall Pub and Parlor toward the end of Federal Hill in Providence. I had been invited to the Ocean State for a luncheon with labor leaders the following day in April 2013 to discuss a series of articles I had written in Forbes about the state pension. Tammany Hall is a great pub and, better still, a rare classic cigar bar—not a modern-day Man Cave devoid of social vitality. In this pub, there was a lot more talking than smoking.

Buddy had read my Forbes articles and having heard about my coming to town, he wanted to hear—from the horse's mouth—what the controversy was all about.

"Buddy Cianci, Rhode Island's most popular talk radio show host on WPRO 630, would like to buy you a drink," I was told by my host. As luck would have it, I happen to enjoy a good weekly cigar and Manhattan and this night of the week seemed as good as any.

The articles I had written detailed a diabolic scheme State Treasurer Gina Raimondo had master-minded to cut pension benefits promised state workers by 3%—supposedly to make the pension more sustainable. What she neglected to tell the public was that she had secretly agreed to increase the investment fees paid to Wall Street hedge fund and private equity billionaires by a corresponding amount.

Wall Street darling Raimondo's so-called "pension reform" was nothing more than a massive wealth transfer backed by her powerful out-of-state financial pals. While Wall Street's solution to every problem is (and has always been) PAY US MORE, paying higher fees is no way to make a state pension more sustainable—trust me. Buddy knew.

That night Buddy was both friendly and engaging, yet through the smoke and flowing alcohol, he was intensely focused.

Buddy was aware that all Rhode Islanders had been swept into the controversy regarding the sustainability of the state and local pensions and he sincerely wanted to know how the facts I had uncovered would change the debate. More than a talk show host pursuing a scoop, he cared.

He asked whether I could appear on his radio talk show at rush hour the following day and on his taped Sunday television show. He sensed that this out-of-towner was "on to something." Over the past few years, I have regularly been invited to return to Buddy's radio show, updating the public on my newest investigative findings.

No one else cared that there might be another side to the story crafted by state leaders—only Buddy.

As much as conventional Rhode Island politicians may have scorned him, the people of Rhode Island knew he cared about them and they couldn't help but care about him too—no matter what. Believe it or not, "people skills" do matter even today—far more than debating finesse, or an impressive resume.

Buddy may not have always acted with the public's best interests in mind, but, by today's standards, he would likely be considered Rhode Island's least dangerous politician. Any corruption he may have been involved with amounted to chump-change. He never dared to sell the state out to Wall Street, costing billions.

Like so many others, I will miss him.

EDWARD SIEDLE

The Greatest Retirement Crisis in American History

Forbes, March 20, 2013

We are on the precipice of the greatest retirement crisis in the history of the world. In the decades to come, we will witness millions of elderly Americans, the Baby Boomers and others, slipping into poverty. Too frail to work, too poor to retire will become the "new normal" for many elderly Americans.

That dire prediction, which I wrote two years ago, is already coming true. Our national demographics, coupled with indisputable glaringly insufficient retirement savings and human physiology, suggest that a catastrophic outcome for at least a significant percentage of our elderly population is inevitable. With the average 401(k) balance for sixty-five-year-olds estimated at $25,000 by independent experts—$100,000 if you believe the retirement planning industry—the decades many elders will spend in forced or elected "retirement" will be grim.

Corporate America and the financial wizards behind the past three decades of so-called retirement innovations, most notably titans of the pension benefits consulting and mutual fund 401(k) industries, are down-playing just how bad things are already and how much worse they are going to get.

Americans today are aware that corporate pensions have been virtually eliminated and that the few remaining private, as well as the nation's public pensions, are in jeopardy. Even if you are among the lucky few that have a pension, you cannot rest assured that it will be there for all the years you'll need it. Whether you know it or not, someone is busy trying to figure how to screw you out of your pension.

Americans also know the great 401k experiment of the past thirty years has been a disaster. It is now apparent that 401ks will not provide the retirement security promised to workers. As a former mutual fund legal counsel, when I recall some of the outrageous sales materials the industry came up with to peddle funds to workers, particularly in the 1980s, it's almost laughable—if the results weren't so tragic.

There was the "Dial Your Own Return" cardboard wheel of fortune that showed investors which mutual funds they should select for any given level of return. Looking for 12%? Load up on our government plus or option income funds! It was that easy to get the level of income needed in retirement, investors were told.

The signs of the coming retirement crisis are all around you. Who's bagging your groceries: a young high school kid or an older "retiree" who had to go back to work to supplement his income or qualify for health insurance?

The impending crisis will come in what I call "waves," as opposed to a tsunami hitting all at once. With each successive wave, more elderly will be drowned. The older you are, the harder it is to recover from a set-back.

Wave 1: Retirees Come Back To Work

Workers who retired post-2000 realize they cannot possibly live on their meager retirement savings, virtually no interest, and limited health benefits, and conclude they must go back to work full-time. For example, one of my clients, a sheriff's office, has already seen retirees coming back to work largely for health insurance coverage. While these retirees do have pensions, the cost of health insurance, when not subsidized by an employer, is far greater than they had anticipated. For those who are physically and mentally capable of going back to work and are welcomed by their former employers or other employers, this is a plausible survival strategy.

Wave 2: Workers Delay Full Retirement

Many current workers realize they have not saved enough to retire and postpone retirement for a certain number of years. They still believe, however, that someday they will be able to retire and live off their savings. This strategy makes sense for workers who can hang onto their jobs at the same (or better) pay and are healthy enough to keep working. On the other hand, older workers who are forced by employers to agree to demotions, pay cuts, or part-time status to stay on, may feel demoralized.

Wave 3: Full Retirement Is Unachievable

Many current workers and retirees at some point realize that they can never fully retire, i.e., stop working altogether, and commit to working part-time for as many of their golden years as possible.

The problem is, of course, that each year more elderly people become too frail to work and fewer employers are interested in hiring them, even on a part-time basis. Remember those ads that said, "It's hell to be forty and out of work?" Try looking for work at seventy or eighty.

Wave 4: Drowning

At some point, lack of savings, lack of employment possibilities, and failing health will catch up with the overwhelming majority of the nation's elders. Let me emphasize that we're talking about the overwhelming majority, not a small percentage who arguably made bad decisions throughout their working lives.

Given the certainty that a retirement crisis is headed toward our shores, you'd think that our elected officials would be hard at work preparing a response. Of course, that's not happening. To the contrary, conservatives are trying to pare back so-called entitlements that will mushroom in the near future and liberals have failed to acknowledge the crisis or propose any solutions.

Eventually the pain will be so widespread that the crisis will be impossible to ignore. For many, the challenge is to hang in there until help arrives.

Wealthy Clients Should Beware of Private Banks

Forbes, May 24, 2010

It's a little-known secret that many wealthy investors are profoundly dissatisfied with the private banks that oversee their assets. They should be. Private banking is an investment backwater where appearances and reputations often far exceed capabilities.

To make matters worse, as private banks become more embedded in their clients' overall financial lives, firing even poorly performing ones becomes challenging. The bank may, for example, become your lender or serve as a corporate trustee in your family trust. Separating lending, asset management, corporate trustee duties, and other services among best-of-class firms is almost always the wiser course.

For those who are unfamiliar with private banking, it seeks to cater to high-net-worth clients—often those with $10 million or more to manage—by blending menus of bank, investment management, and other financial services. "Private" refers to the notion that customer service is provided on a highly personalized basis and delivered by employees who are supposed to be highly trained financial advisors.

Harris Private Bank offers advice on managing wealth, investments, trusts, and estates, as well as other family office services. If you feel overwhelmed by "the various facets of wealth," you can "partner with experienced advisors" who will "advocate on your behalf," according to Harris. Specialized knowledge of income and estate tax planning, retirement planning, philanthropy, risk management, wealth transfer, and business succession are all readily available, its promotional literature says.

Before signing on, investors should ask whether private banks can offer all these services on competitive terms. After all, private banking services are supposed to be the top of class—reserved for those who can afford the very best.

It might be due to the conservative nature of banking culture, or due to the way bank employees are paid, but clients and potential clients should bear in mind that few private banks have earned distinction as top-performing asset managers. This may not be a concern if you honestly believe Citi Private Bank, for example, in claiming to "scour the ranks of top-tier managers to offer our clients the most suitable equity, fixed income, private equity, hedge fund, and real estate managers." To be comfortable you're getting the best deal going from a private bank, you must also be confident that it's not stuffing your account with investments based not on the prospect of strong performances but mainly because they're managed by the bank or its affiliates.

In reality, private banking is riddled with conflicts of interests involving the use of proprietary products and cross-sold services. Less common is full disclosure to investors of the potential harm such practices may do to their wealth. If you opt to let a private bank handle your affairs, you can expect your separately managed accounts to be filled with proprietary products from the bank itself or from affiliated mutual funds, hedge funds, and money market funds.

This arrangement allows the bank to earn multiple layers of fees—often one for overseeing your overall portfolio and others for managing the sub-accounts. Such captive selling is highly entrenched. When a client who'd asked me to look into how her money was being managed asked her private bankers to invest in a hedge fund she'd become interested in on her own, she was told her relationship required that all her assets be invested in funds selected by the bank itself. Otherwise, of course, the bank risked cutting itself out of the fees that outside managers in such programs typically kick back to the bank.

Bank-affiliated mutual funds are rarely good performers either. If fund selection were based on investment merit alone, these dogs wouldn't stand a chance.

Performance information and analysis routinely provided in the money management industry, meanwhile, is often curiously lacking in the reports private-bank clients receive. Products internally managed by the bank that do not report their performance to third-party databases may be sold without any meaningful information provided to the investor.

Among the information that's often lacking: assets under management in the product; identity, qualifications, and even location of portfolio managers; and performance history gross and net of all fees compared to relevant benchmarks. Instead, projected or hoped-for returns are often used to sell proprietary products. Clients who rely solely on bank projections of future returns are usually setting themselves up for disappointment or outright disaster.

Borrowing money from a private bank that holds your investments raises a host of concerns, ranging from whether it will offer the best lending rates and terms to whether it will face conflicts of interest, or exert leverage over your affairs, in the event you run into problems paying it back. What's more, armed with intimate knowledge of clients' finances, and driven by the fees to be earned cross-selling, private banks may propose lending programs that dramatically and inappropriately increase the risks individuals face.

Using a private bank as a corporate trustee for your family trusts also presents problems. Beneficiaries of trusts established decades ago may get stuck with corporate trustees whose identities have changed over time as a result of mergers, acquisitions, or the sale of trust departments. The current trustee may bear no resemblance to the trustee the family patriarch selected decades ago.

Unlike with money managers who are registered as investment advisors under federal or state securities laws, trust banks may be able to change advisors without even giving clients notice. Older trusts may lack provisions for removal of the corporate trustee, other than via a lawsuit alleging gross negligence or more serious wrongdoing. Without full disclosure, it may be impossible for beneficiaries to uncover even egregious conduct that would give rise to removing a trustee. Even if they discover horrific investment performance on the trustee's part, that alone may not be reason enough to fire the trustee.

All this leaves beneficiaries with no one to turn to when it comes to addressing their complaints. Worse, even if beneficiaries do unearth misconduct, the trustee usually has the power to tap the principal and income of the trust in defending himself. That means the beneficiaries are in effect forced to fund the opposition.

Another reason to avoid private bank wealth managers is that neither the firms nor their employees are required to register with the Securities and Exchange Commission as investment advisors or investment advisory representatives. Private bank investors may not receive the same disclosure that they would from SEC registered advisors—information that may be critical to effective investment decision-making.

Similarly, background and disciplinary information of the sort that the Financial Industry Regulatory Authority provides via its BrokerCheck program may not be available regarding the private banking employees who handle money. In short, the individuals with primary responsibility for investors' assets, however well-groomed, may possess no credentials or experience in investment matters.

To date, lack of transparency and powerful social networking has protected private banks from harsh review. That may change post-Madoff as more wealthy customers scrutinize the quality of the supposedly red-carpet services they receive from these tony institutions and the related investment results. Private banks make sense if you're willing to pay through the nose for the plush carpeting and fine china—but don't kid yourself into thinking private banks will provide you with world-class fiduciary guidance or superior investment results. Most won't.

State Pension Boards Lack Investment Experience: What Could Possibly Go Wrong?

Forbes, May 24, 2020

In the United States, the combined value of pension plan assets held by state and local governments is over $4 trillion. These pensions are overseen by boards of trustees comprised of lay men and women who generally lack any knowledge or expertise in investment matters. There are a few state and local laws which require one or more board members of public pensions to possess some financial experience but such requirements are extremely rare.

Typically, public pension boards include some individuals, such as active or retired teachers, cops, firefighters, and sanitation workers, who are supposed to represent the interests of workers and pensioners. Other board members are appointed by politicians, such governors and mayors who are supposed to represent the interests of voters, aka taxpayers.

Again, typically none of the worker or political representatives knows anything about investing—yet they decide how trillions in public pension assets are invested.

What could possibly go wrong, you might ask?

Everything and far more than you can imagine.

For example, with $354 billion in assets under management, the California Public Employees Retirement System, America's largest state pension, has historically been considered the "gold standard" for public pensions in its investment approach, its integrity, and its management.

How well is the nation's "best of the best" American public pension managed?

In 2016, the former chief executive of the pension was sentenced to a prison term of 4.5 years after pleading guilty to a conspiracy charge for taking more than $250,000 in cash and other bribes from his friend and former CalPERS board member Alfred Villalobos. Prosecutors said Villalobos, who killed himself weeks before he was due to stand trial, reportedly made $50 million as a middleman for investment firms looking to get a piece of CalPERS' business.

Later that same year, a former director of New York's massive public pension was charged with accepting crack cocaine, money for prostitutes, and other lavish bribes to steer more than $2 billion in securities trades.

Preet Bharara, US attorney for the Southern District of New York said at the time, "The hard-earned pension savings of New Yorkers should never serve as a vehicle for corrupt, personal enrichment. The intersection of public corruption and securities fraud appears to be a busy one, but it's one that we are committed to policing."

A recent study of US public pensions concluded that oversight of these funds is vitally important to government officials, plan participants, and taxpayers. The effectiveness of pension boards depends on their structure, composition, size, and member tenure. Most important, better board composition is associated with a higher ten-year investment return on fund assets. Hardly surprising.

Members of public pension boards and pension staff may be crooked for hustling cash, hookers, and blow, but they're Boy Scouts compared to the wolves of Wall Street who make billions selling their latest high-cost, high-risk, complex, and opaque deals to unsophisticated public pensions.

When it comes to stealing from Main Street, no one does it better than Wall Street.

Corporate or private pensions are generally no better off than government pensions. Usually someone from the Human Resources or Finance Department has been assigned responsibility for the neglected pension but it's not his or her full-time job.

(I remember a deposition when the Chief Financial Officer responsible for overseeing a multi-billion-dollar corporate pension sheepishly admitted after repeated aggressive questioning that he only spent ten percent of his time on pension matters.)

By the way, Human Resources experience is scarcely relevant to pensions and even corporate finance isn't very helpful.

Pensions are unique and complex. I don't think it's too much to ask that the person safeguarding your retirement savings, as well as the savings of thousands or millions of workers, have some special training.

Fortunately, there are globally-recognized experts in pensions and investments who offer sound advice on how pensions should be prudently managed.

You'd think pension overseers, especially financially-illiterate public pension boards, would listen to these experts. As I explain in my book, Who Stole My Pension? you'd be wrong.

Top Ten Reasons Why Stealing from State and Local "Public Pensions" Is the Perfect Crime

Forbes, November 27, 2017

With assets of over $4 trillion as of Q2 2017, these retirement systems have boatloads of money—a few million, or even billion, stolen won't be missed.

Public pensions are overseen by boards of trustees comprised of laymen utterly lacking any knowledge or expertise in investment or fiduciary matters. Few state or local statutes require public pension board members to meet any minimal standards related to pensions. Time and again, even local hucksters successfully pull the wool over these guys' eyes. When Wall Street comes-a-calling on public pensions, fuggetaboutit.

Public pensions are subject to politicization. The composition of boards and the decisions made by boards regarding pension investments are generally tainted by political considerations. Grease the right politician and you're in like Flint.

While generally subject to state public records laws mandating transparency, these funds are so defensive about the decisions they make and skilled at thwarting public disclosure requirements that a scammer need not be concerned about being exposed.

Public pensions are not subject to the Employee Retirement Income Security Act of 1974 (ERISA), the federal law that establishes minimum standards for pension plans in private industry. ERISA was enacted to protect the interests of employee benefit plan participants and their beneficiaries by requiring the disclosure of financial and other information concerning the plan to beneficiaries; establishing standards of conduct for plan fiduciaries; and providing for appropriate remedies and access to the federal courts. Since ERISA doesn't apply, a would-be thief need not be concerned with any of the preceding.

Public pensions are regulated by a thin patchwork quilt of state and local laws. Many of the most significant issues related to managing pensions are unanswered in these statutes. Anything that's not clearly illegal under applicable law, you can probably get away with.

No federal or state regulator or law enforcement agency is policing these plans for criminal activity. No worries about the Department of Labor or FBI, and even state attorney generals are reluctant to get involved due to political concerns mentioned above.

Many public pensions are not audited annually by independent certified public accountants. State auditors lacking expertise in complex foreign investment schemes may not be up to the task of ferreting out wrongdoing.

Ever-growing percentages of public pension assets are being swept into offshore accounts and illiquid, hard-to-value assets. Nobody's checking to see if the money is even there.

As long as taxpayer rage is focused upon the amount of money flowing into public pension plans and the supposedly "rich" benefits they pay to state and local retirees, investment scamming will not be a priority.

Trust me—whatever you steal won't be missed for years to come.

EDWARD SIEDLE

Rhode Island State Pension May Never Be Able to Exit Gina Raimondo Loser

Forbes, March 7, 2019

Can Rhode Island ever exit the dismally performing investment sold to the state pension in 2006, by former General Treasurer, current Governor Gina Raimondo before she entered politics? Probably not—unless 80% of the investors in the fund (including friends and family of Raimondo)—someday agree to end it. Don't be surprised if the final accounting of this investment is delayed until Raimondo safely exits Rhode Island politics.

As I wrote last month, recently the state pension was told by Raimondo's Point Judith Capital that it will have to remain in the floundering investment for a thirteenth straight year, even though the state's initial $5 million, ten-year commitment had long expired.

The pension was scheduled to exit Raimondo's fund in 2016 but the firm, supposedly exercising its discretion under a secret agreement the state supposedly signed, unilaterally extended the life of the investment in 2017 and again in 2018.

In late 2018, General Treasurer Seth Magaziner surprised pension stakeholders by announcing a new reason for delaying termination of the investment yet another year. Magaziner disclosed, for the first time, the 2006 secret agreement the pension signed with Point Judith allowed Raimondo's fund to hold onto state money another year if 80 percent of investors agree.

The very fact that an investment, shrouded in secrecy and foisted on the state pension by the now-governor, has continued to lose money for the pension and pay money to Raimondo for the past thirteen years—with no end in sight—should demand enhanced disclosure and public scrutiny, in my opinion.

Thankfully, according to Magaziner, his "Transparent Treasury initiative has made the Rhode Island pension system a national leader in pension transparency." The Prince of Transparency should welcome probing questions, right?

So, for the past month I have been asking Treasurer Magaziner's office questions about the most recent extension of the life of the Raimondo fund. Magaziner's spokesman, Evan England, has failed to answer almost all my questions. Let's call it the "not-so-transparent treasury."

In response to the following questions:

When did the pension become aware of the most recent (2019) extension?

What evidence does the pension possess documenting that 80% of investors in the fund voted to extend?

Who are the other investors in the fund?

How many of the other investors are, like Raimondo, insiders of the fund?

Do the agreements the state entered into with Point Judith permit additional extensions of the life of the fund? If so, how many extensions are permitted and under what circumstances?

Did the pension vote against extension of the life of the Point Judith fund or simply abstain from voting?

What was the projected liquidation value of the investment at 12/31/18, had termination and liquidation been demanded by the limited partners?

The Treasurer's office has merely responded:

We did not support the amendment, but enough limited partners to amend the contract did.

It is our policy and practice to disclose key information about the state's investments to the public. The only exception is in instances where we are duty-bound, as fiduciaries, to maintain the confidentiality of information that could cause material harm (emphasis added) to the fund and, by extension, our members.

Wow! The Treasurer is "duty-bound" to keep secret the governor's deal with the state pension? Disclosure would cause "material harm" to state workers?

How exactly would pension participants—state workers whose Cost of Living Adjustments (COLAs) were cut to pay fees to Raimondo's former investment firm—be harmed by exposure/disclosure?

As one of the nation's leading experts on pension fiduciary duties, I fail to see how, once the Treasurer has already disclosed the life of the Point Judith fund could be extended for yet another year with 80% investor approval, disclosing whether additional extensions are permitted could possibly cause material harm to the fund or its participants.

By the way, it is my understanding from speaking with experts who regularly draft limited partnership agreements, with 80% investor approval, it is likely the fund could continue, and pay fees, forever to Raimondo. Magaziner ain't sayin.

I wrote to Magaziner's flack,

"Help me, if you can, understand the Treasurer's reasoning. Indeed, in my expert opinion, there is a compelling case that the Treasurer's profound lack of transparency regarding this failing, politically-charged, dark money investment is utterly unjustifiable. To my knowledge, the Raimondo investment is unique. There is no other investment in the state's portfolio that was sold to it by the current Governor, former Treasurer."

Stakeholders deserve an answer to when, if ever, the pension can exit this loser.

Draconian Cradle-To-Grave Provisions in Private Equity, Real Estate Funds Common

Forbes, March 25, 2019

Draconian "cradle-to-grave" provisions in private equity and real estate funds, permitting investment managers to extend fund lifetimes and charge investors fees virtually forever, are commonplace—yet almost universally overlooked by even so-called sophisticated public pensions. Rhode Island Treasurer Seth Magaziner, championing "financial literacy" at high schools across the state, seemingly has no problem with the state pension paying Governor Gina Raimondo's former firm indefinitely for private equity underperformance. How many other private equity and real estate investments in the nation's public pension portfolios, such as CalPERS, have similarly harsh cradle-to-grave provisions?

Earlier this month I wrote that it seemed unlikely the Rhode Island state pension would ever be able to exit the dismally performing $5 million investment sold to the pension in 2006, by former General Treasurer, current Governor Gina Raimondo before she entered politics. Rhode Island Treasurer Seth Magaziner's office failed to answer my repeated questions regarding whether the agreements the state had entered into permitted additional extensions of the life of the fund and, if so, how many extensions were permitted and under what circumstances? I concluded that unless 80% of the investors in the fund (including friends and family of Raimondo)—someday agree to end it, Rhode Islanders shouldn't be surprised if the final accounting of this investment was delayed until Raimondo safely exited Rhode Island politics.

The Raimondo investment is unique in that there is no other investment in the state's portfolio that was sold to it by the current Governor, former Treasurer.

However, Rhode Island's state pension is chocked full of many other private equity and real estate funds which may have similar cradle-to-grave provisions. We can't know for sure because

Treasurer Magaziner will not permit public scrutiny of the relevant fund agreements. State secrets, it seems.

Worse still, severely underfunded public pensions across the nation are gambling heavily on private equity funds seemingly unaware their assets may be locked-in for fifty years or more. Last week, California Public Employees' Retirement System, the nation's largest public pension fund voted to move forward with a plan that could add another $20 billion in private equity investment into the portfolio—supposedly as a means to improve investment returns and overcome increasing pension liabilities.

Mark Renz, Chief Investment Officer at Socius, a multi-family office in Fort Lauderdale, offers prospective clients "transparency reviews" focusing on fees, expenses, and risks. Renz has seen private equity and real estate funds which have cradle-to-grave provisions permitting the investments to continue for up to fifty years. Worse still, most of these funds have no absolute limitations—they can go on forever.

"Most people don't really know what they own or signed up for. When I tell them they may be stuck for a lifetime—generally when performance is suffering—nobody's happy. The risks related to cradle-to-grave provisions are almost never discussed with investors."

David Darby, Managing Partner at DG Wealth Partners in Palm Beach Gardens, also advocates transparency reviews for prospective clients and shares Renz's concerns. "Obviously, it is in the General Partner's financial interest to extend the life of the fund until performance improves and in the meantime the GP profits by continuing to collect fees. Heads, the GP wins; tails, the LPs lose—whether performance improves or not.

The problem is most acute," says Darby, "in fund of funds which are popular among retail investors. Fund of funds, which invest in dozens of underlying funds, almost guarantee the retail investor will be locked-in for far longer than he anticipated."

Despite long claiming to be the gold standard, the very fact that CalPERS, a massively underfunded state pension, is taking such a wild private equity gamble should be cause for alarm, in my opinion. Gamblers who double-down usually crash and burn. More worrisome, other public pensions gambling in private equity and real estate are even less savvy.

Rhode Island Public Pension Reform: Wall Street's License to Steal

Forensic Investigation of the Employee Retirement System of Rhode Island for Rhode Island Council 94, American Federation of State, County, and Municipal Employees by Benchmark Financial Services, Inc., October 17, 2013.

Executive Summary

Two years ago, Rhode Island's state pension fund fell victim to a Wall Street coup. It happened when Gina Raimondo, a venture capital manager with an uncertain investment track record of only a few years—a principal in a firm that had been hired by the state to manage a paltry $5 million in pension assets—got herself elected as the General Treasurer of the State of Rhode Island with the financial backing of out-of-state hedge fund managers. Raimondo's new role endowed her with responsibility for overseeing the state's entire $7 billion in pension assets.

In short, the foxes (money managers) had taken over management of the henhouse (the pension).

For Raimondo, a forty-two-year-old Rhode Island native, serving as state treasurer represents a major career boost. It also has presented her with an opportunity to enrich herself and her hedge fund backers at the expense of the state's pension fund, the public workers who are counting on it to finance their retirements, and the taxpayers who could be stuck for millions, or billions, of dollars if it's mismanaged.

Further, a significant portion of the Treasurer's wealth and income relates to shares she owns in two illiquid, opaque venture capital partnerships she formerly managed at Point Judith Capital—one of which she convinced the state to invest in on different, less favorable terms. Unlike the state which paid millions for its shares in one of the Point Judith funds, the Treasurer was granted shares in both of the venture capital funds for free.

Worse still, the venture capital industry is noted for its lack of transparency and once the Treasurer assumed office she refused to disclose virtually any information regarding the investment fund in which she and the state pension remain co-investors.

For example, the Treasurer refused to release documents which would reveal whether she (or any other investor) had been granted any special rights more favorable than those granted to the state, or other limited partners in the fund.

Point Judith Capital, the Treasurer's former employer, is a firm which is substantially funded by Tudor Investment Corp., a multi-billion-dollar private equity and hedge fund conglomerate controlled by the secretive billionaire Paul Tudor Jones. Without Tudor as a strategic partner possessing a substantial investment performance history, Raimondo's Point Judith would not have been a contender for a $5 million venture capital commitment from the state.

In a very real sense, today Rhode Island's leading investment fiduciary is largely compensated by an out-of-state hedge fund investor—worse still, she is paid indirectly and secretly. The myriad unique conflicts of interest and risks related to this unprecedented state of affairs have not been thoroughly investigated or addressed.

Transparency and accountability have suffered as the pension has increased its allocation to hedge, venture capital, and private funds to almost $2 billion or twenty-five percent and the Treasurer has withheld most information about these high-risk, high-cost investments from both the State Investment Commission, a ten-member volunteer body that is chaired by the General Treasurer and oversees the investments of the state pension, and the general public. Ironically, in Rhode Island, limitations on public access to records have grown in the Information Age.

The Treasurer has emerged as the leading national advocate of a disingenuous form of public pension "reform" which involves slashing worker's benefits and thwarting public access to information regarding the riskiest of pension investments while, in secret, dramatically increasing the risks to retirement plans and the fees they pay to Wall Street. A report she produced in 2011 titled "Truth in Numbers: The Security and Sustainability of Rhode Island's Retirement System" made a stark case for the pension overhaul and benefits cuts she envisioned, while notably omitting details regarding the greater costs and risks related to her plans for restructuring the Fund's investment portfolio.

Benchmark Financial Services, Inc. ("Benchmark") was retained by Rhode Island Council 94 of the American Federation of State, County, and Municipal Employees, AFL-CIO, to provide a preliminary expert forensic review of the investment program at the Employee Retirement System of Rhode Island ("ERSRI" or "the Fund"). We were also asked to examine whether the Treasurer's so-called reform agenda was actually enhancing the security and sustainability of ERSRI and the true costs and risks of the sweeping changes she has implemented.

- **Treasurer's Lack of Transparency**

Forensic investigations of pensions require access to evidence. It is fair to say that the Office of the General Treasurer of the State of Rhode Island, through its actions has made conducting this review on behalf of participants in the Fund far more difficult.

There has been a sinister pall of secrecy regarding fundamental investment information related to the ERSRI (such as the level of investment advisory, performance, and other fees paid for money management, the risks related to hedge, private equity, and venture capital strategies and investments, and conflicts of interest) orchestrated by state officials and aided by key investment services providers, punctuated by periodic self-serving misrepresentations regarding such investment matters to the general public.

The overwhelming majority of the information Benchmark requested for this review from the General Treasurer pursuant to the Rhode Island Access to Public Records Act (APRA) has been withheld in apparent violation of state law; the Treasurer claims the state is contractually obliged to defer to the money managers it has hired on the release of supposedly proprietary information. The worst is yet to come since the Treasurer has deliberately withheld the most potentially damaging information we have requested.

Most disturbing, from a regulatory and public policy perspective, is that the General Treasurer's practice of withholding information and intentionally providing incomplete disclosures regarding ERSRI's investments results in: (1) misleading the public as to fundamental investment matters, such as the true costs and risks related to investing in hedge, private equity, and venture capital funds; (2) understating the investment expenses and risks related to ERSRI; and (3) misrepresenting the financial condition of the state of Rhode Island to investors.

For these reasons, it is recommended that this report, in general, be provided to securities regulators and law enforcement for appropriate action. However, other specific matters identified herein, i.e., apparent blatant illegalities involving billions in retirement assets nationally, such as hedge funds secretly profiting at the expense of public pensions across the country, demand an immediate, focused response by securities regulators and law enforcement, in our opinion.

Recently, four open-government groups—Common Cause Rhode Island, the state's chapter of the American Civil Liberties Union, the Rhode Island Press Association, and the League of Women Voters of Rhode Island released a letter to the Treasurer voicing their concerns regarding the Treasurer's strategy of withholding hedge fund records. These groups believe that since the financial reports are paid for with public funds and detail how the state is investing the public's money, they should be made public in their entirety; further they found "troubling" the Treasurer's decision to allow the hedge funds to decide what information to release.

The groups should be alarmed—secrecy is critical to the Treasurer's pension "reform" wealth transfer scheme and she is, in effect, rewriting the rules applicable to public access to state investment information in Rhode Island to accomplish this objective.

- **So-Called Pension Reform Scheme Permanently Reduces Benefits To Retirees**

The Rhode Island Retirement Security Act of 2011, enacted November 18, 2011, suspended the Cost of Living Adjustment ("COLA") for all state employees, teachers, state police, and judges, until ERSRI's funding level for all groups, calculated in the aggregate, exceeds 80 percent.

Under the new law, the COLA is targeted at two percent and will be calculated by subtracting 5.5 percent from ERSRI's five-year average investment returns and will range from 0 to 4 percent.

Whether retirees receive any COLA will depend upon both ERSRI's funding level and the Fund's actual investment returns—both of which are volatile, unpredictable, and subject to manipulation by elected officials and others. The manipulation of both of these key goalposts has already begun.

In April 2011, the State Retirement Board lowered the state's assumed rate of return from 8.25 percent to 7.5 percent. A recent new report by an actuarial firm hired by the Treasurer concluded that the State Retirement Board should "consider lowering" the assumed 7.5 percent rate of return even further. To the surprise of even the actuarial firm issuing the new report, the Treasurer claimed the suggestion that the reduced assumption of 7.5 percent may be too optimistic was "terrific news…the numbers are accurate."

The Treasurer has publicly stated that the investment assumption will be reviewed next summer and has acknowledged that the impact of any such future reduction on ERSRI's funding level could "be big." Based upon reliable sources, it is our understanding that the actuaries have agreed to strategically recommend, over time and in steps, further reducing the investment assumption to 6 percent—massively increasing ERSRI's underfunding.

As the investment assumption has been ratcheted downward increasing ERSRI underfunding, the investment expenses have been manipulated upward.

The staggering, almost 700 percent planned increase in ERSRI's investment expenses (disclosed to date) from $11 million to an estimated $70 million—fees paid to Wall Street hedge fund and other alternative managers—has and will continue to drag down net investment returns, further reducing the likelihood of a COLA payment.

Worse still, the investment performance of the Fund has lagged behind its peers under the new mix of assets adopted at the Treasurer's urging in recent years, earning a mere 11.07 percent versus 12.43 percent for the median public-sector pension during the twelve months ended June 30, 2013. If the hedge fund managers continue to perform as badly as they have to date, the damage to ERSRI will be substantially greater—hundreds of millions annually.

In summary, the likelihood that any meaningful COLA will ever be paid in the future under the new statutory scheme is remote—a fact which has not been shared with workers and retirees.

On the other hand, the so-called pension reform scheme as executed by the Treasurer (gorging on hedge, private equity, and venture capital funds), guarantees investment-related fees paid to Wall Street will continue to climb to approach $100 million—an outcome which was both foreseeable and foreseen, i.e., intentional.

Most revealing, the projected cost to ERSRI of the Treasurer's $2 billion alternative investments gamble over the next twenty years amounts to in excess of $3 billion and far exceeds the COLA savings the Treasurer has projected—another inconvenient truth that, to date, has been withheld from the public.

Public pension reform, in Rhode Island, amounts to a transfer of worker's wealth dollar-for-dollar to Wall Street.

- **SEC Should Investigate ERSRI's Failure to Disclose Skyrocketing Investment Expenses**

The investment management expenses disclosed in ERSRI financial reports to date have been grossly understated by the

Treasurer. While retirement plan fiduciaries are required to monitor the reasonableness of plan fees and expense, the Treasurer initially indicated, when asked, that she did not know the amount of fees ERSRI paid to its investment managers.

Further, since these financial reports provided to the State Investment Commission which oversees the pension materially understate fees, the Treasurer has ensured the SIC cannot possibly and has not ever reviewed whether the fees the ERSRI pays to its hedge, private equity, and venture capital managers are reasonable or excessive.

The Treasurer has intentionally withheld from the public and the SIC information about the soaring investment fees which is material in assessing both whether ERSRI should invest in costly alternative investments and whether benefit cuts are necessary to improve pension funding.

In our opinion, based upon our knowledge of pension investment operations, an investigation by state or federal securities regulators would reveal intentional withholding of material information and misrepresentations regarding state pension costs, as opposed to a lack of knowledge about the exponential growth and magnitude of the fees.

Given the myriad fees related to alternative investments; the industry's lack of transparency and pervasive conflicts of interest, as well as the Treasurer's unwillingness to disclose total fees promptly, the ERSRI investment expenses for FY 2012, which over the past six months have been disclosed by the Treasurer as growing from $10.6 million; to $33.1 million; then $43.3 million, continue to be materially understated.

Further, ERSRI investment expenses for FY 2013, which have been estimated by the Treasurer as growing from $11.5 million; to $47.5 million; then $70 million, continue to be materially understated.

The additional expenses, which remain undisclosed to date, combined, can easily exceed two percent annually—in addition to the already excessive two percent asset-based and twenty percent performance fees alternative investment managers typically charge—adding tens of millions to ERSRI's already soaring disclosed annual investment expenses.

In conclusion, ERSRI's total investment expenses may already, or in the near future, amount to a staggering almost $100 million annually— an amount far in excess of the $5 million cost of conservatively indexing or passively managing the Fund's assets.

- **Lose-Lose: Alternative Investments Both Reduce Returns and Increase Risk**

The Treasurer early on stated that superior investment performance justifies the high fees hedge funds charge; however, as ERSRI's reported investment performance has continued to significantly lag behind its peers, the Treasurer has acknowledged that her new investment strategy utilizing hedge funds could reduce the upside potential for ERSRI's investments.

The loss of upside return at ERSRI is apparent at this time, as the Fund has underperformed the market by hundreds of millions of dollars in the past year alone according to the financial statements; however, the amount of any potential downside protection afforded by the alternatives is unproven and unknown. Thus, it is impossible for the fiduciaries of the Fund, i.e., the State Investment Commission, to assess whether the massive cost related to any supposed risk reduction is reasonable.

In order to determine whether the hedge fund investments owned by ERSRI lower the pension's risk (as the Treasurer has repeatedly represented), Benchmark reviewed the offering memoranda related to many of these investments obtained from independent sources—since the Treasurer refused to provide the documents.

The Treasurer's representations regarding the level of risk related to ERSRI's hedge fund investments are wholly inconsistent with the hedge fund managers' own words. The offering documents prominently warn that an investment in a hedge fund is speculative, involves a high degree of risk, and is only suitable for persons who are willing and able to assume the risk of losing their entire investment—hardly an appropriate investment for a public pension plan.

While ERSRI's hedge funds generally disclose specific risks related to investment strategies they may pursue, the managers have wide latitude to invest or trade their fund's assets, and to pursue *any* particular strategy or tactic deemed advisable by the manager—all without obtaining ERSRI approval.

Since the managers may completely change their investment strategies at any time, there is no way ERSRI can ensure that the hedge funds are providing any diversification whatsoever—contrary to representations by the Treasurer. For example, all the hedge fund managers could invest in a single asset class, say cash, or a single stock, say Enron, at an inopportune time.

- **ERSRI Agrees To Be Kept In The Dark, Grants Mystery Investors Licenses to Steal and Consents To Potential Nondisclosure Illegalities**

The offering documents of the hedge funds reveal that investors, such as ERSRI, agree to permit hedge fund managers to withhold complete and timely disclosure of material information regarding ERSRI's investment in their funds. In the words of one manager, investors "will not have the objective means by which to evaluate its operation or to determine whether it is being followed…further, investors may not have the ability to review the investment positions."

Shockingly, ERSRI fiduciaries have consented to being kept in the dark, abrogating their duty to monitor and safeguard pension assets.

Worse still, ERSRI agrees to permit the hedge fund managers to retain absolute discretion to provide certain mystery investors with greater information about investment strategies and portfolio holdings and the managers are not required to disclose such arrangements to ERSRI. As a result, the hedge fund managers expressly warn that ERSRI is at risk that other unknown investors may profit at its expense.

The absolute discretion ERSRI has granted to certain managers amounts to a license to steal from the state pension.

Finally, the offering documents warn that the hedge fund nondisclosure policies may violate applicable laws, including, but not limited to Rhode Island's.

The above outrageous nondisclosure policies detailed in the hedge fund offering documents cause these investments to be, at a minimum, inherently impermissible for a public pension, such as ERSRI, if not illegal.

However, given that public pension investments in alternative investments have doubled in recent years (now amounting to twenty-four percent of portfolios) and billions in public pension assets across the country are currently at risk from such hedge fund schemes, the need for an immediate, focused response by securities regulators and law enforcement is compelling.

Finally, the identity of any mystery investors that may be permitted by managers to profit at ERSRI's expense, as well as any relationships between these investors, the Treasurer, or other public officials, should be investigated fully by law enforcement and securities regulators—especially since leading hedge fund insiders have financially supported the pension "reform" that gave rise to these hedge fund hirings and related mysterious arrangements.

- **Heightened Risks Related To Hedge Fund Offshore Regulation And Custody**

Some of the hedge funds in which ERSRI invests are incorporated and regulated under the laws of foreign countries, presenting additional, unique risks. There is no evidence the State Investment Commission was aware of, or ever considered, the unique risks related to foreign regulation of hedge funds.

Likewise, since ERSRI's alternative investment assets are held at different custodian banks located around the world, as opposed to being held by ERSRI's master custodian, the custodial risks are heightened and should have been considered by the State Investment Commission.

When a member of the SIC requested information regarding the names and locations of ERSRI's hedge fund custodians recently, Chief Investment Officer Anne-Marie Fink responded, "We don't have a single document that lists all the funds and all the custodians." Obviously, if ERSRI did not have such a document, the SIC could not have ever reviewed the many different custodians for safety and soundness.

While withholding such important investment information regarding hedge funds from the SIC may make it easier for the Treasurer to claim such information is proprietary and deny public record requests consistent with her pension "reform" agenda, it effectively undermines the SIC's ability to oversee ERSRI's riskiest investments.

- **SEC Should Investigate Questions Surrounding ERSRI's Point Judith Venture Investment**

It appears that the 2.5 percent asset-based and 20 percent performance fees paid to Point Judith by ERSRI are significantly higher than the then venture capital industry standard of 2 percent asset-based and 20 percent performance fees. Since Point Judith Capital was a small, unproven manager at the time of the investment by ERSRI, there is no reason to believe the firm should have commanded a higher fee. The limited records provided indicate that Tudor's track record and expertise were paramount in the Point Judith Capital proposal to ERSRI; absent Tudor as a strategic partner and investor, Point Judith would not have been able to compete for a $5 million venture capital allocation from ERSRI.

The Treasurer has made numerous public statements regarding the performance of the Point Judith II fund, as well as released summary performance figures which are strikingly divergent. Based upon incomplete information she has provided, the performance of the investment has ranged from her initial claim of

22 percent, to 12 percent, to 10.9 percent, to 6.2 percent, to 4 percent, to -16.7 percent.

In conclusion, as a result of the Treasurer's refusal to publicly disclose all of the material information regarding Point Judith Capital and the Point Judith II fund she formerly managed and sold to ERSRI, choosing instead to disclose limited unverified information which is wildly inconsistent, it is impossible for the general public, participants, and taxpayers to assess her and the firm's investment capabilities, as well as whether ERSRI should have ever invested, or should remain invested, in the Point Judith II fund.

This lack of disclosure is especially troubling since it is our understanding that Point Judith Capital is soliciting investors at this time for a new investment fund. To the extent that any investment information publicly disseminated regarding past performance of the firm, or its funds, is inaccurate, potential new, as well as existing investors may be misled.

In order to prevent any possible confusion or misleading of investors, it is appropriate to refer this matter to the SEC for investigation.

- **Rhode Island Ethics Commission Opinion and "Blind Trust" Fail to Address Conflicts Regarding Point Judith Investment**

In a letter to the Rhode Island Ethics Commission requesting an advisory opinion concerning whether she had taken sufficient steps to avoid conflicts of interest relative to her ties to a venture capital fund in which the state had made an investment, the Treasurer represented that in 2007 the State Investment Commission entered into a ten-year contract with Point Judith in which the State agreed to invest $5 million dollars in the Point Judith II fund.

She also represented that the State's investment in the fund was passive, meaning that after signing the contract with Point Judith and making its investment commitment, the State Investment

Commission had no say in the fund's ongoing management or investment decisions.

The Treasurer notably failed to mention in her letter to the Ethics Commission that the state had not merely entered into a ten-year contract with Point Judith. Rather, the state was a limited partner in a fund managed by Point Judith as General Partner and, as a limited partner the state may have broad rights in the fund's ongoing management, or investment decisions, the exercise of which may conflict with her rights and interests.

Further, as a Point Judith insider, she, or other investors, may have been granted special rights more favorable than those granted to the state, including special withdrawal rights; rights to receive reports from the partnership on a more frequent basis or that include information not provided to other limited partners; rights to receive reduced rates of the incentive allocation and management fee; rights to receive a share of the incentive allocation, management fee, or other amounts earned by the general partner or its affiliates. If true, the Treasurer may literally be profiting at the expense of the state.

Since the Treasurer has refused to disclose documents related to the Point Judith II fund, as well as her and ERSRI's investment in the fund, the public cannot know whether permitting the co-investment to continue is harmful to the Fund. Regardless, the characterization of the investment in the Point Judith II Fund as merely a ten-year contract in a passive investment as to which the state had no say is neither complete nor accurate.

In order to create further separation from her investment in the Point Judith funds, the Treasurer represented that prior to assuming office she placed all her right, title, and interest in both funds into a blind trust designated as the Raimondo Blind Trust. While a blind trust may be of value in certain circumstances, where, as here, the sole assets of the trust, i.e. the shares in the two Point Judith funds, are illiquid, i.e. cannot be sold for a decade, no protection is afforded. The purpose of the blind trust is to keep the beneficiary unaware of the specific assets of the trust, so as to avoid a conflict of interest between the beneficiary and the investments.

In this case, the Treasurer knows precisely the assets held in the Blind Trust during her entire term as Treasurer and continues to enjoy cash distributions related to the Point Judith funds— payments exponentially greater than her state salary in the past year—and payments related to shares she was granted for free.

Rather than provide protection against conflicts, here the blind trust serves to enable the conflict of interest involving ERSRI to persist throughout her term.

Most important, in connection with granting the Advisory Opinion, the Treasurer did not indicate, and Ethics Commission did not consider, that the Treasurer would subsequently refuse to disclose to the public information regarding ERSRI's investment in Point Judith II.

Ironically, the Blind Trust scheme she proposed to the Ethics Commission coupled with her nondisclosure policy regarding the Point Judith II fund, has resulted in only the public being "blind" as to the Point Judith II fund.

In short, in our opinion, this arrangement constitutes a misuse of the blind trust device.

- **SEC Should Investigate ERSRI Investment Consultant Conflicts, Payments From Money Managers**

The investment consultant retained by ERSRI to provide objective, independent advice regarding alternative investments, Cliffwater LLC, has disclosed in its regulatory filings with the SEC that it receives compensation from the very investment managers it recommends or selects for its clients. The amount and sources of such compensation have not been disclosed to ERSRI or anyone else and Cliffwater has changed its disclosure regarding such payments in its

SEC filings during the course of this review, as a result of recent questions we have raised.

Further, Cliffwater representatives have admitted elsewhere that the firm receives an undisclosed amount of compensation from at least one prominent ERSRI manager, Brown Brothers Harriman—a firm which manages approximately $272 million for the ERSRI and is also a private equity manager.

Based upon responses to records requested, it is apparent that ERSRI has never asked Cliffwater for detailed information necessary to evaluate potential conflicts of interest related to payments received from money managers, such as the names of the managers and amounts paid to Cliffwater. While the effort related to investigating any such conflicted payments to Cliffwater is minimal, the potential harm to the pension if Cliffwater's recommendations have been tainted is enormous.

Cliffwater's substantial investment manager client-base, recent changes to its SEC disclosures, and inconsistent statements made by representatives of the firm to public pension trustees all constitute, in our opinion, "red flags." Given the SEC's past regulatory focus on pervasive pension consultant industry conflicts of interest, a referral for investigation by the SEC is warranted.

- **"Pay To Play" Placement Agent Abuses at ERSRI**

Contrary to the Treasurer's public statements prior to this investigation, undisclosed placement agent fees were paid by ERSRI's investment managers to intermediaries or middlemen for selling their investment products to ERSRI.

In response to our APRA request, the Office of the General Treasurer indicated that ERSRI had received a confidential inquiry from the SEC regarding placement agents on May 8, 2009. The state's response to the SEC indicated, at the outset, that ERSRI had not undertaken any independent investigation of the facts stated therein.

Given that the role and compensation of placement agents had become a highly controversial issue nationwide by 2009 and that the risks, as well as potential recoverable fees and damages related to placement agents were significant, the lack of any meaningful fiduciary response, i.e., an independent, thorough investigation, by ERSRI to the SEC inquiry was, in our opinion, inexcusable.

Rather than undertake an independent investigation, ERSRI relied upon advice provided by its then private equity consultant, Pacific Corporate Group Asset Management. At the very time ERSRI was relying upon PCG for objective, independent advice regarding controversial placement agent fees under scrutiny by regulators and law enforcement, it was revealed in published reports (which were easily accessible to ERSRI), that PCG itself was embroiled in a national pay-to-play scandal involving the firm's relationship with former CalPERS board member turned placement agent, Alfred Villalobos. Villalobos, who reaped more than $58 million in placement agent fees, was indicted for fraud earlier this year.

The Fund has not in the years following the SEC inquiry undertaken any subsequent independent investigation to verify the full extent of any placement agent fees paid and related damages, or sought to recover even the known placement agent fees, or consulting fees paid to PCG for objective, as opposed to tainted, advice.

Given that the advice the pension received from PCG was, at a minimum, conflicted and potential violations of law may exist, in our opinion, a subsequent independent investigation should have been undertaken.

Recently, over $1 million in secret placement agent fees (which were previously confidentially disclosed to the SEC) have finally been disclosed to the public by ERSRI in response to our APRA requests. Most flagrant, the largest placement agent fee disclosed ($437,500)—paid to a highly controversial agent (Diamond Edge)—related to an investment as to which ERSRI's private equity consultant, PCG, had also received millions in placement agent fees. There was absolutely no need to pay any-one hundreds of thousands of dollars to "introduce" PCG or ERSRI to the investment that PCG was already familiar with. The squandering of these placement agent fees has never been investigated by ERSRI.

On September 20, 2013, AFSCME agreed to pay ERSRI $2,385.00 for additional information regarding placement agent fees that the Treasurer's office has refused to provide for free.

It is highly likely, in our opinion that additional fees were paid in the past that have not been disclosed to the SEC, or anyone else, by ERSRI. In the event that there are additional undisclosed placement agent fees at ERSRI, regulators and possibly law enforcement should be notified.

CPSIA information can be obtained
at www.ICGtesting.com
Printed in the USA
BVHW040059260422
635013BV00004B/10